Ninja Foodi 2-Basket Air Fryer Cookbook for Beginners

The Complete Guide of Ninja Foodi 2-Basket Air Fryer| 800-Day Easy Tasty Recipes| Air Fry, Broil, Roast, Bake, Reheat, Dehydrate and More

By Kamilia Jones

Table of Contents

Introduction

What is the Ninja Foodi 2-Basket Air Fryer?

The Ninja Foodi 2- Basket Air Fryer is the next revolutionary appliance coming from the awesome folks working at Ninja Kitchen! No matter how unbelievable the concept might sound, Ninja Kitchen has put on countless hours of engineering into crafting this meticulously designed appliance that takes the Air Frying game to a whole different level.

At its heart, the Ninja Foodi 2 Basket Air Fryer is a simple and exceedingly effective Air Fryer that gives you all the basic functions that you would expect from an Air Fryer. With this appliance, you can Air Frye, Bake, Broil, Dehydrate, Air Crisp, and more! You know, the usual Air Fryer stuffs.

However, what makes this unique is the super cool "Dual Zone" technology that completely flips the game in the Air Frying market.

If you are looking to cut down your cooking to half, or you want to make two different meals at the same time. The same appliance, then the Ninja Foodi Dual Zone/ 2 Basket Air Fryer is exactly what you need!

Simply put, the Dual Zone technology allows the appliance to be put on either single cook mode or multi cook mode.

Single cook mode works as usual; you cook using just a single basket. However, with the Dual Cook mode, you can seamlessly set the different timer, mode, and temperature for both of the zones individually and cook the meals you require.

Alternatively, you may give the same settings to both of the zones and cook the same meal in a doubled portion without spending any more time than you would need when making just a single portion.

While handling two Air Fryer baskets might sound a little bit complicated at first, the way how Ninja Kitchen has engineered this appliance has made it extremely accessible and easy to handle.

Understanding the functional buttons and features

The Dual Zone Air Fryer technology of this appliance has merged 6 different cooking functions such as Air Broil, Air Fry, Roast, Bake, Dehydrate and Reheat into one simple and easy to the appliance.

This appliance is extremely awesome for people who love the bake and cook crispy foods.

This particular Air Fryer comes with 2 different Fryer baskets, which are marked as 1 and 2. each should be inserted into their respective section of the appliance because of their different shapes.

Keep in mind that the baskets themselves don't have any buttons, so you can just pull them out and insert them as needed.

The display itself is divided into 2 different sections that indicate each section of the Basket settings. Pres Key -1 on the control panel to select Basket 1 setting and Key 2 for basket 2 settings.

Apart from that, the other functional buttons that you should know about include:

- **Air Broil:** This mode will allow you to give your meals a nice crispy finish and melt toppings of the food.
- **Air Fry:** This is the standard mode that you should use if you want to cook/fry food without using oil
- **Roast:** This essentially turns your appliance into a roaster oven that allows you to cook soft and tender meat
- **Bake:** This will allow you to bake awesome delicious desserts and treats
- **Reheat:** This will allow you to re-heat and warm your leftover meals

- **Dehydrate:** This feature will allow you to dehydrate meats, fruits, and vegetables.
- With the function buttons out of the way, the next thing you should focus on is the appliance's operating buttons.
- **Temp Key:** The Up and Down keys will allow you to adjust the cooking temperature.
- **Time Arrows:** The Up and Down keys here will allow you to adjust the cooking time.
- **SMART FINISH button:** This button will allow your appliance to automatically sync the times of both cooking zones and let them finish simultaneously.
- **MATCH COOK button:** This button will allow you to automatically match the settings of Zone 2 with that of Zone 1. This is amazing when you want to cook many cooks or a large portion of the same food.
- **START/PAUSE button:** These buttons will allow you to initiate, stop, and resume your meal's cooking.
- **POWER BUTTON:** This button is pressed to turn the appliance on and off when needed.
- **Hold Mode:** The Hold sign will appear on the display screen in the SMART FINISH mode. When the cooking time of one zone is greater than the other, the hold will appear for the zone with less cooking time as it will wait for the cooking of another zone to be complete.

Learning the functions work

To properly use the Ninja Foodi 2 Basket Air Fryer, you should have a good idea of the different cooking programs present in the appliance. While the previous section covered the different available functions, this section will tell you how to use them. We will go through them one by one.

Air Broil
- The first step is to insert the crisper plate in your cooking basket, add ingredients into the Basket and insert the Basket into the unit

- By default, the unit will use Zone 1; however, if you want to use zone 2, you need to select Zone 2
- Select the AIR BROIL cooking mode
- Use the TEMP keys to set the temperature that you need
- Use the TIME key to set your desired time
- Press the START/PAUSE button to start cooking
- Once the cooking is done, you will hear a beep, and an "End" sign will appear on the display
- Remove the cooked ingredients and serve

Air Fry

- The first step is to insert the crisper plate in your cooking basket, add ingredients into the Basket and insert the Basket into the unit
- By default, the unit will use Zone 1; however, if you want to use zone 2, you need to select Zone 2
- Select the AIR FRY cooking mode
- Use the TEMP keys to set the temperature that you need
- Use the TIME key to set your desired time
- Press the START/PAUSE button to start cooking
- Once the cooking is done, you will hear a beep, and an "End" sign will appear on the display
- Remove the cooked ingredients and serve

Bake

- The first step is to insert the crisper plate in your cooking basket, add ingredients into the Basket and insert the Basket into the unit
- Select the BAKE cooking mode
- Use the TEMP keys to set the temperature that you need
- Use the TIME key to set your desired time
- Press the START/PAUSE button to start cooking
- Once the cooking is done, you will hear a beep, and an "End" sign will appear on the display

- Keep in mind that you can reduce the temp by 25 degrees F while converting the traditional oven recipes for Air Fryer baking
- Remove the cooked ingredients and serve

For the other cooking modes available, the process is pretty simple. You will the same steps, select the crisper plate/cooking rack as needed, select the required mode, zone, and temperature then start cooking.

Keep in mind, though, that the broiling function is not available for the MATCH COOK technology, as the appliance only allows you to broil food in one Basket at a time. If you have many ingredients to broil, the best way is to broil in batches.

Thanks to the Dual-Zone technology, you have access to other exclusive features of the appliance.

MATCH COOK

If you want to cook a large amount of the same food, or you want to cook two different foods at the same time, here are the steps to follow:

- Add your cooking ingredients into the Basket, insert both baskets into the unit
- Zone 1 will stay lit; press your desired function button. Use the TEMP buttons to set the temperature, use the TIME key to set the desired time.
- Press the MATCH COOK button to copy the settings of basket 1 to that of basket 2
- Press the START/PAUSE button and initiate cooking in both baskets
- Once done, the "' End" sign will appear on both screens

SMART FINISH TECHNOLOGY

These functions will allow both of the cooking zones to complete their cooking simultaneously, even if both of the zones have completely different cook settings.

- Add listed ingredients to your Basket and then insert the baskets into the Air Fryer unit
- Press the Smart Finish Mode, and the machine will automatically sync during cooking
- At first, Zone 1 will stay illuminated. At this point, you need to choose the cooking function for this zone; use the TEMP key to fix temperature and TIME to set the time.
- Now select Zone 2, set the cooking function
- Use TEMP Keys to set temperature and Time key to set the cooking time for Zone 2.
- Once all is set, press the start button; the timer will start ticking for both of the zones according to the set timer, the cooking will finish simultaneously.
- On Smart Finish Mode, you can also start cooking simultaneously and let it end at different times. For that, simply select the cooking time and press the start button for both Zones

Hearty tips for using the appliance

Since this is a relatively new appliance to hit the market, people are still beginning to grasp this amazing appliance's full potential. They are exploring how to properly use this product. The following tips will greatly enhance your cooking experience with this appliance and make everything a breeze.

- While most of the required temperatures are already provided in the recipes, if you ever feel confused, just have a look at the cooking table provided in this book.
- It's always suggested that you collect all of the ingredients you require before starting your cooking session. If you are unable to find a specific ingredient, then make sure to find an alternative beforehand. The recipes in this book already have the best ingredients chosen to provide the best flavor. Still, since different people have different

taste buds, you might consider altering a few if you feel like it.

- Make sure to read the recipes thoroughly before you start cooking; if you find any step confusing, then do a simple google search to properly understand the steps.
- Before starting your cooking session, make sure that your appliance to clean and free from any dirt or debris. Follow the steps provided in the section below if you are confused about how to do it.
- The Air Fryer location is extremely important if you want your meals to cook evenly since it relies heavily on the airflow. Therefore, make sure to keep it in a space where it has enough space to "Breath" in Air and cook the meals properly.
- If you are using frozen food, you should consider thawing them before putting them in your Air Fryer basket.
- Since the Air Fryer relies on Superheated Air to do the cooking, make sure to never overcrowd the cooking baskets. Always keep space in between heavy ingredients. Now that you have two zones to work with, this shouldn't be a problem at all!
- When cooking with the Air Fryer, it is always advised that you opt for organic ingredients. Try to find the freshest ones possible as they will give you the best flavors.
- When choosing a baking tray for your Air Fryer, try to go for lighter color trays/dishes. Dark colors such as black ones would absorb more heat that might result in uneven cooking.

Maintaining and cleaning the appliance

Despite having a bucket load of functions under its hood, cleaning up and maintain the Ninja Foodi 2 Basket Air Fryer is relatively easy. To clear up any confusion that you may have, let me break down the process into very simple and easy to follow steps.

- First of all, unplug the appliance before you start cleaning it, making sure that you have given it enough time to let it cool

- Next, remove the Air Fryer baskets from the main appliance and keep them on the side; this will help with the cooling process as well
- Once they are cool, remove the Air Crisper plates and wash them thoroughly
- Take the Air Fryer baskets and use soapy water to clean them; make sure to avoid using any hard scrubber as they might damage the surface
- The Air Fryer racks can be washed in Dishwasher; afterward, use a soft scrub to gently clean any food stuck to the sides
- Take the main unit, and gently wipe it using a clean piece of cloth
- Once everything is clean, return the Basket back to the Air Fryer
- And now, you are ready to go!

If you just follow these simple steps, you will be able to keep your 2 Basket Air Fryer in tip-top shape for days to come!

Air Fryer cooking time table

Below you will find a rough breakdown of the general cooking time required for various ingredients when using the Air Fryer. Since this is a double zoned Air Fryer, you will be able to cook double the amount of ingredients simultaneously by adding double the amount of ingredients to the two zones of the Air Fryer.

Meat

	Cooking Temperature (Fahrenheit)	Cooking Time (Minutes)
Bacon	350	8-12
Chicken (Whole)	350	45-65
Chicken Breasts (Bone-In)	375	25-35
Chicken Breasts	350	15-20

(Boneless)		
Chicken tenders	350	8-12
Chicken Thighs(Bone-In)	400	15-22
Chicken Thighs(Boneless)	375	16-21
Chicken Wings	375	18-28
Lamb(Leg)	375	18-28
Lamb(rack)	375	10-17
NY Strip steak	400	8-14
Pork Chops	350	10-15
Pork Tenderloin	375	15-25
Ribeye/T-Bone	400	15-25

Ground Meat

	Cooking Temperature (Fahrenheit)	Cooking Time (Minutes)
Burger Patties(1/4 1b)	350	8-15
Meatballs	375	6-9
Sausages(raw)	375	15-20
Sausages(cooked)	375	7-12

Chopped Sea/Food

	Cooking Temperature (Fahrenheit)	Cooking Time (Minutes)
Chicken	400	8-15
Pork	375	8-12
Steak	400	8-12
Salmon	400	6-12
Tilapia	350	6-10

Others

	Cooking Temperature (Fahrenheit)	Cooking Time (Minutes)
Banana. sliced	375	6-8
Chickpeas	400	12-17
Tofu, cubed	375	12-17
Tortilla chips	350	3-8
Pizza, personal size	375	7-12

Frozen Food

	Cooking Temperature (Fahrenheit)	Cooking Time (Minutes)
Chicken tenders, breaded and pre-cooked	375	14-18
Dumplings/Potstickers	350	6-10
Egg rolls	400	8-14
Fish sticks	400	8-12
French fries	325	14-17
Hash browns	325	6-9
Mini pizzas	375	8-15
Mozzarella sticks	375	7-10
Onion rings	400	8-10
Tater Tots	400	10-15

Vegetables

	Cooking Temperature (Fahrenheit)	Cooking Time (Minutes)
Broccoli	400	5-9

Brussels Sprouts, halved	375	9-16
Butternut squash, chopped	400	15-20
Carrots, chopped	400	10-15
Cauliflower. whole	350	15-20
Cauliflower, chopped	400	10-15
Corn on the cob	400	8-10
Eggplant	400	15-18
Green Beans	400	8-10
Kale leaves	375	4-5
Mushrooms, Button	375	8-13
Mushrooms, Portobellos	350	10-12
Okra	350	12-14
Onions. sliced	400	8-10
Parsnips, chopped	375	10-16
Peppers, small	400	4-8
Potatoes, whole	400	30-45
Potatoes, chopped	375	15-30
Sweet potatoes, chopped	400	8-15
Sweet Potatoes, whole	375	30-245
Tomatoes, cherry	350	5-8
Tomatoes, halved	350	6-12
Zucchini, chopped	350	8-12
Zucchini. noodles	400	10-20

Chapter 1: Brunch Recipes

Perfect Breakfast Sausage

Prep Time: 10 minutes/ Cook Time 12 minutes/ Serves: 4

Ingredients:

- 1 pinch sriracha flakes
- 1 pinch salt and pepper
- 1 teaspoon olive oil
- 8 whole eggs
- 2 bell pepper, halved, seeds removed

Directions:

1. Divide the sausages in the two Air fryer baskets.
2. Return the Air Fryer Baskets to the Air Fryer.
3. Select the Air Fryer mode for Zone 1 with 390 degrees F temperature and 13 minutes cooking time.
4. Press the MATCH COOK button to copy the settings for Zone 2.
5. Initiate cooking by pressing the START/PAUSE BUTTON.
6. Serve warm and fresh.

Nutritional Contents:

Calories: 187
Carbohydrate: 8g
Protein: 24g
Fat: 6g

Cinnamon And Pineapple Grill

Prep Time: 10 minutes/ Cook Time 5 minutes/ Serves: 4

Ingredients:

- 1 teaspoon cinnamon
- 5 pineapple slices
- 1/2 cup brown sugar

Directions:

1. Make a mix of cinnamon with brown sugar.
2. Cover the pineapple slices with the mixture.
3. Let the pineapple slices rest for 20 minutes.
4. Divide the pineapple slices between the two zones
5. Set the temperature of zone 1 to 340 degrees F and cook time to 10 minutes
6. Press MATCH COOK to copy settings from zone 1 to zone 2
7. Let it cook for 10 minutes, flip the pineapple slices and cook for 10 minutes more
8. Serve with basil and honey!

Nutritional Contents:

Calories: 480
Fat: 18g
Carbohydrates: 71g
Protein: 13g

Excellent Mushroom And Garlic Flavored Packs

Prep Time: 10 minutes/ Cook Time 10 minutes/ Serves: 4

Ingredients:

- 16 small button mushrooms
- 1 and 1/2 slice white bread
- 1 garlic clove, crushed
- 1 tablespoon flat-leaf parsley, chopped
- Black pepper to taste
- 1 and 1/2 tablespoon olive oil

Directions:

1. Set temperature of Zone 1 of Air Fryer to 390 degrees F, set time to 9 minutes
2. Use MATCH COOK to copy settings from Zone 1 to Zone 2
3. Take a food processor and add bread slices, garlic, pepper, and parsley
4. Grind them up until a crumb-like texture is achieved
5. Add olive oil to the crumb mix and stir well
6. Take your mushrooms and prepare them by cutting off the stalks
7. Fill the cap with the crumb mixture
8. Pat any excess crumbs off
9. Divide the mushrooms between both zones, and let them cook until golden brown
10. Serve and enjoy once done!

Nutritional Contents:

Calories: 240
Carbohydrate: 28g
Protein: 3g
Fat: 14g

Crispy Caramelized Morning Pop Corns

Prep Time: 10 minutes/ Cook Time 15 minutes/ Serves: 6

Ingredients:

- 8 cups popcorn
- 1 cup butter
- 1 cup of sugar
- 1/3 cup whipped cream

Directions:

1. Set temperature of Zone 1 to 240 degrees F and set timer to 5 minutes
2. Click MATCH COOK to copy settings from zone 1 to zone 2
3. Divide the corns between the two zones and cook for 5 minutes
4. Transfer them to a bowl
5. Take a large bowl and put the popcorn in the bowl
6. Mix butter, sugar, and cream and heat over medium heat stirring constantly. The sauce should be boiling; continue boiling until the mixture reaches the softball stage 240^0F.
7. Remove mixture from heat and pour over popcorn, stirring until all popcorn is well coated. Be sure to serve it right away.
8. Enjoy!

Nutritional Contents:

Calories: 120
Fat: 2.5g
Carbohydrates: 25g
Protein: 1g

Cheesed Up Air Sticks

Prep Time: 10 minutes/ Cook Time 8 minutes/ Serves: 4

Ingredients:

- 6 cheese sticks, snake-sized
- 1/4 cup parmesan cheese, grated
- 2 eggs
- 1 tablespoon Italian seasoning
- 1/4 cup flour, whole wheat
- 1/4 tablespoon rosemary, grounded
- 1 tablespoon garlic powder

Directions:

1. Take cheese sticks and set aside
2. Take a shallow bowl and beat eggs into the bowl
3. Mix cheese, flour, and seasonings in another bowl
4. Roll the cheese sticks in the eggs and then in the batter
5. Now do the process again till the sticks as well coated
6. Set temperature of zone 1 to 370 degrees F and time to 7 minutes
7. Select MATCH COOK to copy settings of zone 1 to zone 2
8. Divide the cheese sticks into Baskets and cook
9. Serve and enjoy!

Nutritional Contents:

Calories: 50
Fat: 2g
Carbohydrates: 3g
Protein: 2g

Classic Dutch Pancakes

Prep Time: 10 minutes/ Cook Time 10 minutes/ Serves: 4

Ingredients:

- 3 eggs
- 2 tablespoons unsalted butter
- 1/2 cup flour
- 2 tablespoons sugar, powdered
- 1/2 cup milk
- 1 and 1/2 cups fresh strawberries, sliced

Directions:

1. Set temperature of Zone 1 to 330 degrees F and set bake mode, set timer to 15 minutes
2. Click MATCH COOK to copy settings from zone 1 to zone 2
3. Heat with a 6-by-6-by-2 inch pan in the Basket and add the butter and heat until the butter melts.
4. Take a medium-sized bowl and add flour, milk, eggs, and vanilla.
5. Beat them well with an eggbeater until combined and frothy.
6. Divide the batter between the two baskets, or place the direction of the pan inside if possible
7. Bake for 12 to 16 minutes or until the pancake is puffed and golden brown.
8. Remove from the oven and drizzle them with powdered sugar and strawberries.
9. Serve immediately and enjoy!

Nutritional Contents:

Calories: 196
Fat: 9g
Carbohydrates: 19g
Protein: 16g

Classy Pickle Fries

Prep Time: 10 minutes/ Cook Time 20 minutes/ Serves: 4

Ingredients:

- 24 hamburger dill pickle chips
- 1/3 cup whole-wheat panko breadcrumbs
- 1/4 teaspoon garlic powder
- 1/4 cup (2 large) egg white or fat-free liquid egg
- Dash cayenne pepper
- 1/4 teaspoon onion powder
- Ketchup. to dip
- Dash each salt and black pepper

Directions:

1. Grease the baskets of both zones with a bit of oil
2. Set temperature of Zone 1 to 375 degrees F and set BAKE mode, set timer to 20 minutes
3. Select MATCH COOK to copy settings of zone 1 to zone 2
4. Take a bowl and mix breadcrumbs with seasoning into it
5. Blot pickle chips dry
6. Transfer them into a medium-small bowl
7. Coat with egg whites to both sides
8. Remove the excess eggs and then coat with seasoned
9. Bake for 10 minutes
10. Bake 10 minutes more to make it crispy
11. Serve and enjoy!

Nutritional Contents:

Calories: 59
Fat: 0.5g
Carbohydrates: 11.5g
Protein: 2.5g

Awesome French Toasted Sticks

Prep Time: 10 minutes/ Cook Time 8 minutes/ Serves: 4

Ingredients:

- 1 teaspoon icing sugar
- 1 pinch ground clove
- 1 pinch nutmeg ground
- 1 pinch cinnamon, ground
- 1 pinch salt
- 2 eggs, beaten
- 2 tablespoons butter
- 4 pieces of bread

Directions:

1. Add two eggs to a mixing bowl and stir cinnamon, nutmeg, ground cloves, and salt, then whisk well.
2. Spread butter on both sides of the bread slices and cut them into thick strips.
3. Dip the breadsticks in the egg mixture and place them in the two Air Fryer baskets.
4. Return the Air Fryer Baskets to the Air Fryer.
5. Select the Air Fryer mode for Zone 1 with 390 degrees F temperature and 8 minutes cooking time.
6. Press the MATCH COOK button to copy the settings for Zone 2.
7. Initiate cooking by pressing the START/PAUSE BUTTON.
8. Flip the french toast sticks when cooked halfway through.
9. Serve.

Nutritional Contents:

Calories: 391
Carbohydrate: 36g
Protein: 6g
Fat: 3g

Early Morning Pumpkin Muffins

Prep Time: 10 minutes/ Cook Time 13 minutes/ Serves: 4

Ingredients:

- 1/2 teaspoon nutmeg
- Cooking spray
- 1/2 tablespoons vanilla essence
- 1/2 tablespoon cocoa nib
- 1/2 teaspoon coconut butter
- 1 medium egg, beaten
- 1/4 cup honey
- 1 cup gluten-free oats
- 1/2 cup pumpkin free oats

Directions:

1. Add oats, honey, eggs, pumpkin puree, coconut butter, cocoa nibs, vanilla essence, and nutmeg to a bowl and mix well until smooth.
2. Divide the batter into two 4-cups muffin trays, greased with cooking spray.
3. Place one mini muffin tray in each of the two Air Fryer Baskets.
4. Return the Air Fryer Baskets to the Air Fryer.
5. Select the Air Fryer mode for Zone 1 with 375 degrees F temperature and 13 minutes cooking time.
6. Press the MATCH COOK button to copy the settings for Zone 2.
7. Initiate cooking by pressing the START/PAUSE BUTTON.
8. Allow the muffins to cool, then serve.

Nutritional Contents:

Calories: 138
Carbohydrate: 32g
Protein: 10g
Fat: 10g

Awesome Crispy Egg Rolls

Prep Time: 10 minutes/ Cook Time 13 minutes/ Serves: 4

Ingredients:

- 1 cup of water
- 1 tablespoon olive oil
- 6 egg roll wrappers
- 2 sausage patties
- 1/2 cup cheddar cheese, shredded
- Salt and pepper to taste
- 1 tablespoons milk
- 2 whole eggs

Directions:

1. Grease the same skillet with 1 tsp olive oil and pour the egg mixture into it.
2. Stir cook to make scrambled eggs.
3. Add sausage, mix well and remove the skillet from the heat.
4. Spread an egg roll wrapper on the working surface in a diamond shape position.
5. Add a tbsp of cheese at the bottom third of the roll wrapper.
6. Top the cheese with egg mixture and wet the edges of the wrapper with water.
7. Fold the two corners of the wrapper and roll it, then seal the edges.
8. Repeat the same steps and divide the rolls in the two Air Fryer Baskets.
9. Return the Air Fryer Baskets to the Air Fryer.
10. Select the Air Fryer mode for Zone 1 with 375 degrees F temperature and 13 minutes cooking time.
11. Press the MATCH COOK button to copy the settings for Zone 2.
12. Initiate cooking by pressing the START/PAUSE BUTTON.
13. Flip the rolls after 8 minutes and continue cooking for another 5 minutes.

14. Serve warm and fresh.

Calories: 322
Carbohydrate: 14g
Protein: 17g
Fat: 111g

Perfect Egg Pepper Cups

Prep Time: 10 minutes/ Cook Time 12 minutes/ Serves: 4

Ingredients:

- 1 pinch sriracha flakes
- 1 pinch salt and pepper
- 1 teaspoon olive oil
- 8 whole eggs
- 2 bell pepper, halved and seeds removed

Directions:

1. Slice the bell peppers in half, lengthwise, and remove their seeds and the inner portion to get a cup-like shape.
2. Rub olive oil on the edges of the bell peppers.
3. Place them in the two Air Fryer Baskets with their cut side up and crack two eggs in each half of bell pepper.
4. Drizzle salt, black pepper, and sriracha flakes on top of the eggs.
5. Return the Air Fryer Baskets to the Air Fryer.
6. Select the Air Fryer mode for Zone 1 with 390 degrees F temperature and 18 minutes cooking time.
7. Press the MATCH COOK button to copy the settings for Zone 2.
8. Initiate cooking by pressing the START/PAUSE BUTTON.
9. Serve warm and fresh.

Nutritional Contents:

Calories: 212
Carbohydrate: 14g
Protein: 20g
Fat: 11g

Chapter 2: Beef, Pork, And Lamb Recipes

Amazing Texas Corned Beef

Prep Time: 10 minutes/ Cook Time 40 minutes/ Serves: 4

Ingredients:

- 2 stalks celery
- 1 tablespoon beef spice
- 4 carrots
- 12 ounces bottle of beer
- 1 and 1/2 cups of chicken broth
- 4 pounds corned beef

Directions:

1. Set the Zone 1 temperature to 380 degrees F and timer to 30 minutes
2. Click MATCH COOK to copy zone 1 settings to zone 2
3. Cover beef with beer and let it sit for 20 minutes.
4. Chop carrots and onion.
5. Take a pot and place it over high heat; boil carrots, onion, beef in chicken broth.
6. Drain the boiled meat and divide the meat.
7. Place vegetables on top and cover with spices.
8. Cook for 30 minutes in your fryer.
9. Serve and enjoy!

Nutritional Contents:

Calories: 320
Fat: 22g
Carbohydrates: 10g
Protein: 21g

Broccoli Florets Ala Pork Chops

Prep Time: 10 minutes/ Cook Time 13 minutes/ Serves: 4

Ingredients:

- 2 garlic cloves, minced
- 2 cups broccoli florets
- 1 teaspoon salt, divided
- 1/2 teaspoon garlic powder
- 1/2 teaspoon onion powder
- 1/2 teaspoon paprika
- 2 tablespoons avocado oil
- 2 bone-in pork chops

Directions:

1. Rub the pork chops with avocado oil, garlic, paprika, and spices.
2. Add pork chop to the Zone 1 basket of the Air fryer.
3. Return the Air Fryer Basket to the Air Fryer.
4. Select the Air Fryer mode for Zone 1 with 400 degrees F temperature and 12 minutes cooking time.
5. Add the broccoli to the Zone 2 basket and return it to the unit.
6. Select the Air fryer mode for Zone 2 with 375 degrees F temperature and 13 minutes cooking time.
7. Press the SMART FINISH button to sync the settings with Zone 2.
8. Initiate cooking by pressing the START/PAUSE BUTTON.
9. Flip the pork once cooked halfway through.
10. Cut the hardened butter into the cubes and place them on top of the pork chops.
11. Serve warm with crispy broccoli florets.

Nutritional Contents:

Calories: 340
Carbohydrate: 25g
Protein: 57g
Fat: 20g

Beef Stuffed Squash Delight

Prep Time: 10 minutes/ Cook Time 50 minutes/ Serves: 4

Ingredients:

- 2 spaghetti squashes; pricked
- 2 lb. beef; ground
- Salt and black pepper to the taste
- 6 garlic cloves; minced
- 2 yellow onion; chopped
- 2 Portobello mushroom; sliced
- 48 oz. Canned tomatoes; chopped.
- 2 tsp. oregano; dried
- 1/4 tsp. cayenne pepper
- 1 tsp. thyme; dried
- 2 green bell pepper; chopped

Directions:

1. Put spaghetti squash in your air fryer baskets
2. Set Zone 1 temperature to 350 degrees F and timer to 20 minutes
3. MATCH COOK to copy zone 1 settings to zone 2
4. Transfer to a cutting board, and cut into halves and discard seeds.
5. Heat up a pan over medium-high heat, add meat, garlic, onion, and mushroom; stir and cook until meat browns.
6. Add salt, pepper, thyme, oregano, cayenne, tomatoes, and green pepper; stir and cook for 10 minutes.
7. Stuff squash with this beef mix, introduce in the fryer, and cook at 360 °F for 10 minutes. Divide among plates and serve.

Nutritional Contents:

Calories: 260
Fat: 7g
Carbohydrates: 14g
Protein: 10g

Potatoes And Pork With Green Beans

Prep Time: 10 minutes/ Cook Time 15 minutes/ Serves: 4

Ingredients:

- Salt and pepper to taste
- 1 tablespoon olive oil
- 1 pack, green beans, trimmed
- 3/4 pound small potatoes, halved
- 1 and 1/4 pounds pork tenderloin
- 1/4 teaspoon salt and pepper
- 1/2 teaspoon dried thyme
- 1 teaspoon dried parsley flakes
- 2 tablespoons brown sugar
- 1/4 cup Dijon mustard

Directions:

1. Preheat your Air Fryer Machine to 400 F.
2. Add mustard, parsley, brown sugar, salt, black pepper, and thyme in a large bowl, then mix well.
3. Add tenderloin to the spice mixture and coat well.
4. Toss potatoes with olive oil, salt, black pepper, and green beans in another bowl.
5. Place the prepared tenderloin in Zone 1 Basket.
6. Return this Air Fryer Basket to the Air Fryer.
7. Select the Air Fryer mode for Zone 1 with 390 degrees F temperature and 15 minutes cooking time.
8. Add potatoes and green beans to the second Basket
9. Select the Air Fryer mode for Zone 2 with 350 degrees F temperature and 10 minutes cooking time.
10. Press the SMART FINISH button to sync the settings with Zone 2.
11. Initiate cooking by pressing the START/PAUSE BUTTON.
12. Serve the tenderloin with Air Fried potatoes.

Nutritional Contents:

Calories: 380
Carbohydrate: 33g
Protein: 21g
Fat: 20g

Stroganoff Beef

Prep Time: 10 minutes/ Cook Time 10 minutes/ Serves: 4

Ingredients:

- 2-pound thin steak
- 8 tablespoons butter
- Onion
- 2 cup sour cream
- 16 ounces mushrooms
- 8 cups beef broth

Directions:

1. Add butter to a microwave container and microwave it to melt the butter.
2. Set temperature of Zone 1 to 400 degrees F and time to 10 minutes
3. Press MATCH COOK to copy settings of first Zone to Zone 2
4. Take a bowl and add melted butter, sliced mushrooms, cream, chopped onion, and beef broth.
5. Transfer the steaks to the mixture and let it marinate for 10 minutes
6. Transfer steaks to cooking baskets and bake for 10 minutes.
7. Serve and enjoy!

Nutritional Contents:

Calories: 361
Fat: 16g
Carbohydrates: 11g
Protein: 35g

Mushroom Stir Fry With Lamb Shanks

Prep Time: 10 minutes/ Cook Time 35 minutes/ Serves: 4

Ingredients:

- 3 tablespoons olive oil
- 4 lamb shanks
- 6 garlic cloves
- 3 tablespoons fresh rosemary
- 2 teaspoons salt
- 2 teaspoons pepper
- 6 tablespoons balsamic vinegar
- 4 leeks, chopped
- 1 cup red wine
- 2 red onion, chopped
- 2 red bell pepper, chopped
- 20 mushrooms, chopped

Directions:

1. Season the lamb shanks with salt, pepper, rosemary, and 1 tsp olive oil.
2. Set half of the shanks in each of the Air Fryer baskets.
3. Return the Air Fryer Baskets to the Air Fryer.
4. Select the Air Fryer mode for Zone 1 with 390 degrees F temperature and 25 minutes cooking time.
5. Press the MATCH COOK button to copy the settings for Zone 2.
6. Initiate cooking by pressing the START/PAUSE BUTTON.
7. Flip the shanks halfway through, and resume cooking.
8. Meanwhile, add and heat the remaining olive oil in a skillet.
9. Add onion and garlic to sauté for 5 minutes.
10. Add in mushrooms and cook for 5 minutes.
11. Add red wine and cook until it is absorbed
12. Stir all the remaining vegetables along with black pepper and salt.
13. Cook until vegetables are al dente.
14. Serve the Air fried shanks with sautéed vegetable fry.

Nutritional Contents:

Calories: 609
Carbohydrate: 10g
Protein: 30g
Fat: 50g

Beef And Fennel Platter

Prep Time: 10 minutes/ Cook Time 20 minutes/ Serves: 4

Ingredients:

- 4 tablespoons olive oil
- 2-pound beef, cut into strips
- 2 fennel bulb, sliced
- Salt and pepper to taste
- 2 teaspoon sweet paprika
- 1/4 cup tomato sauce

Directions:

1. Take a pan and place it over medium-high heat, add beef and brown for 5 minutes
2. Add remaining ingredients to the pan and toss well
3. Set your Air Fryer Zone 1 to 380 degrees F, set the timer to 15 minutes
4. Select MATCH COOK to copy Zone 1 to Zone 2 settings
5. Transfer mix to Air Fryer baskets and cook for 15 minutes
6. Serve and enjoy!

Nutritional Contents:

Calories: 246
Fat: 14g
Carbohydrates: 4g
Protein: 15g

Lovely Pesto Beef Bake

Prep Time: 10 minutes/ Cook Time 35 minutes/ Serves: 4

Ingredients:

- 50 ounces potatoes, boiled
- 28 ounces beef, minced
- 46 ounces jar tomato pasta
- 24 ounces pesto
- 2 tablespoon olive oil

Directions:

1. Mash the potatoes in a bowl and stir in pesto.
2. Sauté beef mince with olive oil in a frying pan until brown.
3. Layer a casserole dish with tomato pasta sauce.
4. Top the sauce with beef mince.
5. Spread the green pesto potato mash over the beef in an even layer.
6. Set the Zone 1 of your Air Fryer to 350 degrees F, timer to 35 minutes, and Mode to BAKE
7. Select MATCH COOK to copy settings from ZONE 1 to ZONE 2
8. Once preheated, place the casserole dish in the oven and close its lid.
9. Once done, serve and enjoy!

Nutritional Contents:

Calories: 352
Fat: 14g
Carbohydrates: 15g
Protein: 26g

Beef Kabobs With Pepper

Prep Time: 10 minutes/ Cook Time 20 minutes/ Serves: 4

Ingredients:

- Sat and pepper to taste
- 1/2 onion, squared
- 1 bell pepper, squared
- 8 skewers, 6 inch
- 2 tablespoons soy sauce
- 1/3 cup low fat sour cream
- 1 pound beef chuck, stew meat, cubed

Directions:

1. Whisk sour cream with soy sauce in a medium bowl, then toss in beef chunks.
2. Mix well, then cover to refrigerate for 30 minutes.
3. Thread the beef, onion, and bell peppers over the skewers alternately.
4. Drizzle the salt and black pepper over the skewers.
5. Place half of the skewers in each of the Air Fryer baskets and spray them with cooking oil.
6. Return the Air Fryer Baskets to the Air Fryer.
7. Select the Roast mode for Zone 1 with 390 degrees F temperature and 20 minutes cooking time.
8. Press the MATCH COOK button to copy the settings for Zone 2.
9. Initiate cooking by pressing the START/PAUSE BUTTON.
10. Flip the skewers once cooked halfway through, and resume cooking.
11. Serve warm.

Nutritional Contents:

Calories: 231
Carbohydrate: 20g
Protein: 34g
Fat: 20g

Subtle Beef Cheeseburgers

Prep Time: 10 minutes/ Cook Time 13 minutes/ Serves: 4

Ingredients:

- Thinly sliced red onion, to serve
- Sliced tomatoes, to serve
- Lettuce, to serve
- Mayonnaise, to serve
- 4 hamburger buns
- 4 American cheese slices
- Salt and pepper to taste
- 1 tablespoon soy sauce
- 2 garlic cloves, minced
- 1 pound beef, ground

Directions:

1. Mix beef with soy sauce and garlic in a large bowl.
2. Make 4 patties of 4 inches in diameter.
3. Rub them with salt and black pepper on both sides.
4. Place the 2 patties in each of the Air Fryer baskets.
5. Return the Air Fryer Baskets to the Air Fryer.
6. Select the Air Fryer mode for Zone 1 with 390 degrees F temperature and 13 minutes cooking time.
7. Press the MATCH COOK button to copy the settings for Zone 2.
8. Initiate cooking by pressing the START/PAUSE BUTTON.
9. Flip each patty once cooked halfway through, and resume cooking.
10. Add each patty to the hamburger buns along with mayo, tomatoes, onions, and lettuce.
11. Serve.

Nutritional Contents:

Calories: 548
Carbohydrate: 20g
Protein: 40g
Fat: 22g

Cream And Beef Wine

Prep Time: 10 minutes/ Cook Time 20 minutes/ Serves: 4

Ingredients:

- Beef roast, 3 pounds
- Salt and black pepper to the taste
- Beef stock, 17 ounces
- Red wine, 3 ounces
- Chicken salt, 1/2 tsp.
- Smoked paprika, 1/2 tsp.
- Diced brown onion, 1
- Minced garlic cloves, 4
- Diced carrots, 3
- Diced potatoes, 5

Directions:

1. Create a salt, pepper, chicken salt and paprika mixture in a bowl, stir
2. Rub this mixture on the beef and put it in a big pan that fits your air fryer
3. Set temperature of Zone 1 to 360 degrees F, set timer to 45 minutes and set mode to ROAST
4. Press MATCH COOK to copy information of Zone 1 to Zone 2
5. Add onion, garlic, stock, wine, potatoes, and carrots
6. Place in your air fryer baskets
7. Cook for 45 minutes.
8. Divide and serve into plates

Nutritional Contents:

Calories: 304
Fat: 20g
Carbohydrates: 20g
Protein: 32g

Exciting Pork And Fennel Platter

Prep Time: 10 minutes/ Cook Time 15 minutes/ Serves: 4

Ingredients:

- 3 tablespoons olive oil
- 2 pork chops
- Salt and black pepper to taste
- 1 teaspoon fennel seeds, roasted
- 1 tablespoon rosemary, chopped

Directions:

1. In a bowl, mix the pork chops with the oil, salt, pepper, fennel, and rosemary; toss and make sure the pork chops are coated well.
2. Set the temperature of Zone 1 to 400 degrees F, Set timer to 15 minutes and set Mode to Roast
3. Select MATCH COOK to copy zone 1 information to Zone 2
4. Transfer the chops to your air fryer baskets and cook at 400 degrees F for 15 minutes.
5. Divide the chops between plates and serve.

Nutritional Contents:

Calories: 281
Fat: 11g
Carbohydrates: 17g
Protein: 20g

Elegant Pork Roast

Prep Time: 10 minutes/ Cook Time 55 minutes/ Serves: 4

Ingredients:

- 4 pounds pork loin roast
- Salt and black pepper to taste
- 2 tablespoons olive oil
- 6 tablespoons smoked paprika
- 2 teaspoons liquid smoke
- 2 tablespoons brown sugar
- 4 tablespoons oregano, chopped

Directions:

1. Place all ingredients into a bowl, mix well, and be sure the pork is thoroughly coated.
2. Set the temperature of Air Fryer Zone 1 to 370 degrees F, set timer to 55 minutes and set mode to ROAST
3. Select MATCH COOK to copy information of Zone 1 to Zone 2
4. Transfer the roast to your air fryer cooking baskets and let the timer run out
5. Slice the roast, divide it between plates, and serve.

Nutritional Contents:

Calories: 300
Fat: 12g
Carbohydrates: 22g
Protein: 18g

Potato Pork Satay

Prep Time: 10 minutes/ Cook Time 60 minutes/ Serves: 6

Ingredients:

- 6 tablespoons butter, melted
- 6 potatoes, peeled and sliced
- 1/2 teaspoon dried thyme crushed
- 1/2 teaspoon ground pepper
- 1 teaspoon salt
- 1 teaspoon dried rosemary, crushed
- 4 tablespoons fresh parsley, minced
- 4 carrots, sliced
- 4 leeks, white portion, sliced
- 2 onion, chopped
- 4 pounds boneless pork, diced
- 4 tablespoons canola oil

Directions:

1. Toss the pork cubes with all the veggies, oil, and seasonings in a baking tray.
2. Set the temperature of Zone 1 to 350 degrees F, set timer to 60 minutes and set mode to ROAST
3. Select MATCH COOK to copy information of Zone 1 to Zone 2
4. Transfer the prepared meat to Air Fryer cooking baskets
5. Let them cook until timer runs out
6. Serve and enjoy!
7. Slice and serve warm.

Nutritional Contents:

Calories: 212
Fat: 11g
Carbohydrates: 14g
Protein: 17g

Chapter 3: Fish And Seafood Recipes

Crispy Rice Flour Shrimp

Prep Time: 10 minutes/ Cook Time 20 minutes/ Serves: 4

Ingredients:

- 6 tablespoons flour
- 2 pounds shrimp, peeled and deveined
- 4 tablespoons olive oil
- 2 teaspoon powdered sugar
- Salt and pepper to taste

Directions:

1. Grease the Air Fryer cooking baskets.
2. Set temperature to 325 degrees F of Zone 1, sett timer to 20 minutes
3. Select MATCH COOK to copy settings of Zone 1 to Zone 2
4. Mix rice flour, olive oil, sugar, salt, and black pepper in a bowl.
5. Stir in the shrimp and transfer half of the shrimp to the air fryer baskets.
6. Cook for about 10 minutes, flipping once in between.
7. Dish out the mixture onto serving plates and repeat with the remaining mixture.

Nutrition Contents:

Calories: 299
Fat: 12g
Carbohydrates: 11g
Protein: 35g

Cheesed Up Shrimp Meal

Prep Time: 10 minutes/ Cook Time 20 minutes/ Serves: 4

Ingredients:

- 2 tablespoons fresh lemon juice
- Pepper as needed
- 1/2 teaspoon pepper flakes, crushed
- 1 teaspoon onion powder
- 1/2 teaspoon dried oregano
- 1 teaspoon dried basil
- 2 tablespoons olive oil
- 4 garlic cloves, minced
- 2 pounds shrimp, peeled and deveined
- 2/3 cup parmesan cheese, grated

Directions:

1. Set temperature to 350 degrees F of Zone 1, grease the cooking baskets
2. Select MATCH COOK and copy the settings of Zone 1 to Zone 2
3. Mix Parmesan cheese, garlic, olive oil, herbs, and spices in a large bowl.
4. Arrange shrimp into the Air fryer baskets in a single layer and cook for about 10 minutes.
5. Dish out the shrimps onto serving plates and drizzle with lemon juice to serve hot.

Nutrition Contents:

Calories: 386
Fat: 14g
Carbohydrates: 5g
Protein: 57g

Invigorating Prawn Burgers

Prep Time: 10 minutes/ Cook Time 6 minutes/ Serves: 4

Ingredients:

- 1/2 cup prawns, peeled, deveined, and finely chopped
- 1/2 cup breadcrumbs
- 2-3 tablespoons onion, finely chopped
- 3 cups fresh baby greens
- 1/2 teaspoon ginger, minced
- 1/2 teaspoon garlic, minced
- 1/2 teaspoon red chili powder
- 1/2 teaspoon ground cumin
- 1/4 teaspoon ground turmeric
- Salt and ground black pepper, as required

Directions:

1. Set Zone 1 temperature to 390 degrees F, set timer to 6 minutes
2. Press MATCH COOK to copy settings of Zone 1 to Zone 2
3. Mix the prawns, breadcrumbs, onion, ginger, garlic, and spices in a bo wl.
4. Make small sized patties from the mixture and transfer to the Air fryer basket.
5. Cook for about 6 minutes and dish out in a platter.
6. Serve immediately warm alongside the baby greens.

Nutrition Contents:

Calories: 240
Fat: 2g
Carbohydrates: 37g
Protein: 18g

Coconut Shrimp Meal

Prep Time: 10 minutes/ Cook Time 20 minutes/ Serves: 4

Ingredients:

- Salt and pepper to taste
- 1 pound large shrimp, peeled and deveined
- 1/2 cup panko breadcrumbs
- 1/2 cup sweetened coconut, shredded
- 8 ounces of coconut milk

Directions:

1. Preheat your Vortex Air fryer to 350 o F and grease an Air fryer basket.
2. Set temperature of Zone 1 to 350 degrees F, timer to 20 minutes
3. Select MATCH COOK to copy settings of Zone 1 to Zone 2
4. Place the coconut milk in a shallow bowl.
5. Mix coconut, breadcrumbs, salt, and black pepper in another bowl.
6. Dip each shrimp into coconut milk and, finally, dredge in the coconut mixture.
7. Arrange shrimps between the baskets
8. Dish out the shrimps onto serving plates and repeat with the remaining mixture to serve.

Nutrition Contents:

Calories: 408
Fat: 23g
Carbohydrates: 11g
Protein: 31g

Energizing Greek Mussels

Prep Time: 10 minutes/ Cook Time 10 minutes/ Serves: 8

Ingredients:

- 8 pounds mussels
- Olive oil as needed
- 2 cup white wine
- 4 teaspoons salt
- 4 bay leaves
- 2 tablespoon pepper
- 2 and 1/2 cup flour

- 2 tablespoon onion powder
- 2 tablespoon fenugreek
- 4 tablespoons vinegar
- 10 garlic cloves
- 8 bread slices
- 1 cup mixed nuts

Directions:

1. Set Zone 1 temperature to 350 degrees F, set timer to 10 minutes
2. Select MATCH COOK to copy settings of Zone 1 to Zone 2
3. Take your food processor and add garlic, vinegar, salt, nuts, pepper, and crumbs.
4. Process and add olive oil, process again to make a cream.
5. Take pan over medium heat and boil bay leaves in white wine, add mussels and keep simmering until the mussels have opened up.
6. Clean mussels from shells.
7. Add flour to your cream sauce.
8. Cover mussels with the prepared sauce and flour.
9. Transfer mussels to Fryer and divide them between the baskets and cook for 10 minutes.
10. Serve with fenugreek and enjoy it!

Nutritional Contents:

Calories: 100
Fat: 2g
Carbohydrates: 18g
Protein: 10g

Creative Shrimp Scampi

Prep Time: 10 minutes/ Cook Time 13 minutes/ Serves: 4

Ingredients:

- 1 pound shrimp, defrosted
- 1 tablespoon basil leaf, minced
- 1 tablespoon chive, chopped
- 2 teaspoons red pepper flakes
- 1 tablespoon garlic, minced
- 1 tablespoon lemon juice
- 4 tablespoons melted butter

Directions:

1. Toss shrimp with melted butter, lemon juice, garlic, red pepper, chives, and basil in a bowl.
2. Divide the shrimp in the two Air fryer baskets.
3. Return the Air Fryer Baskets to the Air Fryer.
4. Select the Air Fryer mode for Zone 1 with 390 degrees F temperature and 13 minutes cooking time.
5. Press the MATCH COOK button to copy the settings for Zone 2.
6. Initiate cooking by pressing the START/PAUSE BUTTON.
7. Toss the shrimp once cooked halfway through, and resume cooking.
8. Serve warm.

Nutritional Contents:

Calories: 319
Fat: 20g
Carbohydrates: 23g
Protein: 25g

Glazed Up Juicy Scallops

Prep Time: 10 minutes/ Cook Time 13 minutes/ Serves: 4

Ingredients:

- Salt and pepper to taste
- 3 tablespoons olive oil
- 12 scallops

Directions:

1. Rub the scallops with olive oil, black pepper, and salt.
2. Divide the scallops in the two Air fryer baskets.
3. Return the Air Fryer Baskets to the Air Fryer.
4. Select the Air Fryer mode for Zone 1 with 390 degrees F temperature and 13 minutes cooking time.
5. Press the MATCH COOK button to copy the settings for Zone 2.
6. Initiate cooking by pressing the START/PAUSE BUTTON.
7. Flip the scallops once cooked halfway through, and resume cooking.
8. Serve warm.

Nutritional Contents:

Calories: 279
Fat: 30g
Carbohydrates: 14g
Protein: 10g

Sweetest Salmon Fillets

Prep Time: 10 minutes/ Cook Time 20 minutes/ Serves: 4

Ingredients:

- 1 teaspoon thyme leaves
- 2 garlic cloves, minced
- 2 tablespoons packed brown sugar
- 4 tablespoons wholegrain mustard
- 4 teaspoons extra virgin olive oil
- Fresh ground black pepper
- Sat as needed
- 4 salmon fillets, 6 ounces each

Directions:

1. Rub the salmon with salt and black pepper first.
2. Whisk oil with sugar, thyme, garlic, and mustard in a small bowl.
3. Place two salmon fillets in each of the Air Fryer baskets and brush the thyme mixture on each fillet.
4. Return the Air Fryer Baskets to the Air Fryer.
5. Select the Air Fryer mode for Zone 1 with 390 degrees F temperature and 17 minutes cooking time.
6. Press the MATCH COOK button to copy the settings for Zone 2.
7. Initiate cooking by pressing the START/PAUSE BUTTON.
8. Serve warm and fresh.

Nutritional Contents:

Calories: 349
Fat: 22g
Carbohydrates: 12g
Protein: 35g

Crazy Lobster Tails

Prep Time: 10 minutes/ Cook Time 18 minutes/ Serves: 4

Ingredients:

- 4 lemon wedges
- 2 teaspoons fresh parsley, chopped
- Salt and pepper to taste
- 2 garlic cloves, grated
- 2 teaspoon lemon zest
- 8 tablespoons butter, melted
- 4 lobster tails

Directions:

1. Spread the lobster tails into Butterfly, slit the top to expose the lobster meat while keeping the tail intact.
2. Place two lobster tails in each of the Air Fryer baskets with their lobster meat facing up.
3. Mix melted butter with lemon zest and garlic in a bowl.
4. Brush the butter mixture on top of the lobster tails.
5. And drizzle salt and black pepper on top.
6. Return the Air Fryer Baskets to the Air Fryer.
7. Select the Air Fryer mode for Zone 1 with 390 degrees F temperature and 18 minutes cooking time.
8. Press the MATCH COOK button to copy the settings for Zone 2.
9. Initiate cooking by pressing the START/PAUSE BUTTON.
10. Garnish with parsley and lemon wedges.
11. Serve warm.

Nutritional Contents:

Calories: 348
Fat: 23g
Carbohydrates: 32g
Protein: 41g

Spinach Dredged Scallops

Prep Time: 10 minutes/ Cook Time 13 minutes/ Serves: 4

Ingredients:_

- 3/4 cup heavy whipping cream
- 1 tbsp tomato paste
- 1 tbsp chopped fresh basil
- 1 tsp minced garlic
- 1/2 tsp salt
- 1/2 tsp pepper
- 12 oz frozen spinach thawed
- 8 jumbo sea scallops
- Vegetable oil to spray

Directions:

1. Season the scallops with vegetable oil, salt, and pepper in a bowl
2. Mix cream with spinach, basil, garlic, salt, pepper, and tomato paste in a bowl.
3. Pour this mixture over the scallops and mix gently.
4. Divide the scallops in the Air Fryers Baskets without using the crisper plate.
5. Return the Air Fryer Baskets to the Air Fryer.
6. Select the Air Fryer mode for Zone 1 with 390 degrees F temperature and 13 minutes cooking time.
7. Press the MATCH COOK button to copy the settings for Zone 2.
8. Initiate cooking by pressing the START/PAUSE BUTTON.
9. Serve right away.

Nutritional Contents:

Calories: 341
Fat: 4g
Carbohydrates: 36g
Protein: 30g

Lovely Broiled Tilapia

Prep Time: 10 minutes/ Cook Time 10 minutes/ Serves: 4

Ingredients:

- 4 pounds potatoes, cut into wedges
- 4 tablespoons chipotle seasoning
- 1/2 cup olive oil
- 2 pounds tilapia fillets
- Old bay seasoning as needed
- Canola oil as needed
- Lemon pepper as needed
- Salt to taste
- Butter buds

Directions:

1. Set the temperature of Zone 1 to 400 degrees F, set timer to 10 minutes and set it to BROIL mode.
2. Cover tilapia with oil.
3. Take a bowl and mix in salt, lemon pepper, butter buds, seasoning.
4. Cover your fish with the sauce.
5. Transfer fillets to the Air Fryer cooking baskets
6. Broil fillets for 10 minutes.
7. Serve and enjoy!

Nutritional Contents:

Calories: 177
Fat: 10g
Carbohydrates: 1.2g
Protein: 25g

Chapter 4: Chicken And Poultry Recipes

Honey-Dredged Chicken Drumsticks

Prep Time: 10 minutes/ Cook Time 15 minutes/ Serves: 4

Ingredients:

- 4 chicken drumsticks, skin removed
- 4 teaspoons olive oil
- 4 teaspoons honey
- 1 teaspoon garlic, minced

Directions:

1. Take a resealable bag and add garlic, olive oil, and honey.
2. Add chicken and mix well; allow it to marinate for 30 minutes.
3. Set temperature of Zone 1 to 400 degrees F, set the timer to 15 minutes
4. Select MATCH COOK to copy Zone 1 settings to Zone 2
5. Transfer your chicken to the cooking baskets and cook for 15 minutes.
6. Enjoy!

Nutritional Contents:

Calories: 120
Fat: 3g
Carbohydrates: 21g
Protein: 2g

Veggie Chicken Platter

Prep Time: 10 minutes/ Cook Time 25 minutes/ Serves: 8

Ingredients:

- Salt and pepper to taste
- 2 teaspoon sage, dried
- 1 teaspoon rosemary, dried
- 4 tablespoons olive oil
- 2 cups chicken stock
- 2 celery stalk, chopped
- 8 chicken breast, boneless and skinless
- 6 garlic cloves, minced
- 2 carrots, chopped
- 2 red onion, chopped

Directions:

1. Take two small pans small enough to fits your air fryer baskets; divide all ingredients and toss well.
2. Set temperature of Zone 1 to 360 degrees F, set the timer to 25 minutes
3. Select MATCH COPY to copy settings of Zone 1 to Zone 2
4. Transfer to Air Fryer cooking basket, dividing them equally
5. Cook until the timer runs out
6. Divide everything between plates, serve, and enjoy!

Nutrition Contents:

Calories: 292
Fat: 12g
Carbohydrates: 20g
Protein: 15g

Hearty Caprese Chicken

Prep Time: 10 minutes/ Cook Time 25 minutes/ Serves: 4

Ingredients:

- 6 chicken breasts
- 6 basil leaves
- 1/4 cup balsamic vinegar
- 6 slices tomato
- 1 tablespoon butter
- 6 slices mozzarella cheese

Directions:

1. Pre-heat your Fryer to 400 degrees F.
2. Pre-heat Zone 1 to 400 degrees F, set the timer to 20 minutes
3. Select MATCH COOK and copy Zone 1 settings to Zone 2
4. Take frying and place it over medium heat, add butter and balsamic vinegar and let it melt.
5. Cover the chicken meat with the marinade.
6. Transfer chicken to your Air Fryer cooking baskets and cook for 20 minutes.
7. Cover cooked chicken with basil, tomato slices, and cheese.
8. Serve and enjoy!

Nutritional Contents:

Calories: 740
Fat: 54g
Carbohydrates: 4g
Protein: 30g

Authentic Turmeric Chicken Legs

Prep Time: 10 minutes/ Cook Time 20 minutes/ Serves: 4

Ingredients:

- 4 tablespoons heavy cream
- Salt and pepper to taste
- 2 tablespoons ginger, grated
- 5 teaspoons turmeric powder
- 4 chicken legs

Directions:

1. Place all ingredients in a bowl and mix well.
2. Set temperature of Zone 1 to 380 degrees F, set the timer to 20 minutes
3. Select MATCH COPY to copy settings of Zone 1 to Zone 2
4. Transfer the chicken to your air fryer cooking baskets and divide them
5. Cook for 20 minutes
6. Divide between plates and serve.

Nutrition Contents:

Calories: 300
Fat: 4g
Carbohydrates: 22g
Protein: 20g

Almond Crusted Chicken Nuggets

Prep Time: 10 minutes/ Cook Time 12 minutes/ Serves: 4

Ingredients:

- 4 slices low-sodium whole wheat bread, crumbled
- 1 cup ground almonds
- 2-pound, low sodium boneless, skinless chicken breasts, cut into 1 and 1/2 inch cubes
- 1 teaspoon ground paprika
- 1 teaspoon dried basil
- 2 tablespoon freshly squeezed lemon juice
- 2 egg white

Directions:

1. Preheat the air fryer oven to 400°F (204°C).
2. Set your temperature to 400 degrees of Zone 1, set timer to 12 minutes
3. Select MATCH COOK to copy settings of Zone 1 to Zone 2
4. In a shallow bowl, beat the egg white, lemon juice, basil, and paprika with a fork until foamy.
5. Add the chicken and stir to coat.
6. On a plate, mix the almonds and bread crumbs.
7. Toss the chicken cubes in the almond and bread crumb mixture until coated, then transfer to the air fryer basket.
8. Place the air fryer baskets onto the baking pan and cook until the chicken reaches an internal temperature of 165°F (74°C) on a meat thermometer.
9. Serve and enjoy!

Nutrition Contents:

Calories: 221
Fat: 11g
Carbohydrates: 6g
Protein: 9g

Chili Chicken Wings Delight

Prep Time: 10 minutes/ Cook Time 43 minutes/ Serves: 4

Ingredients:

- 8 chicken wing drummettes
- Cooking spray as needed
- Chicken seasoning of your choice
- 1/4 cup almond flour
- 1/8 cup low-fat buttermilk

Thai Chili Marinade

- 1 and 1/2 tablespoons low-sodium soy sauce
- 1/2 tablespoon sesame oil
- 1/2 tablespoons Sriracha sauce
- 1/2 teaspoon of rice wine vinegar
- 1 green onion
- 1 and 1/2 garlic cloves
- 1/2 teaspoon ginger, minced
- 1 and 1/2 low sodium so the sauce

Directions:

1. Put all the ingredients for the marinade in the blender and blend them for 1 minute.
2. Keep this marinade aside. Pat dry the washed chicken and place it in the Ziploc bag.
3. Add buttermilk, chicken seasoning, and zip the bag.
4. Shake the bag well, then refrigerator for 30 minutes for marination.
5. Remove the chicken drumettes from the marinade, then dredge it through dry flour.
6. Spread the drumettes in the two air fryer baskets and spray them with cooking oil.
7. Return the Air Fryer Baskets to the Air Fryer.

8. Select the Air Fryer mode for Zone 1 with 390 degrees F temperature and 43 minutes cooking time.
9. Press the MATCH COOK button to copy the settings for Zone 2.
10. Initiate cooking by pressing the START/PAUSE BUTTON.
11. Toss the drumettes once cooked halfway through.
12. Now brush the chicken pieces with Thai chili sauce and then resume cooking
13. Serve warm.

Nutrition Contents:

Calories: 388
Fat: 22g
Carbohydrates: 8g
Protein: 45g

Juicy Chicken And Potatoes Medley

Prep Time: 10 minutes/ Cook Time 22 minutes/ Serves: 4

Ingredients:

- 4 slices bacon, cooked, cut into strips
- 3/8 cup cheddar, shredded
- 1/4 teaspoon paprika, optional
- 8 ounces boneless chicken breast, cubed
- 1/8 teaspoon black pepper, optional
- 1 teaspoon seasoned salt
- 1 teaspoon olive oil
- 15 ounces canned potatoes, drained

Directions:

1. Dice the chicken into small pieces and toss them with olive oil and spices.
2. Drain and dice the potato pieces into smaller cubes.
3. Add potato to the chicken and mix well to coat.
4. Spread the mixture in the two Air fryer baskets in a single layer.
5. Return the Air Fryer Baskets to the Air Fryer.
6. Select the Air Fryer mode for Zone 1 with 390 degrees F temperature and 22 minutes cooking time.
7. Press the MATCH COOK button to copy the settings for Zone 2.
8. Initiate cooking by pressing the START/PAUSE BUTTON.
9. Top the chicken and potatoes with cheese and bacon.
10. Return the Air Fryer Baskets to the Air Fryer.
11. Select the Air Broil mode for Zone 1 with 300 degrees F temperature and 5 minutes cooking time.
12. Initiate cooking by pressing the START/PAUSE BUTTON.
13. Repeat the same step for ZONE 2 to broil the potatoes and chicken in the 2nd Basket.
14. Enjoy with dried herbs on top.

Nutrition Contents:

Calories: 378
Fat: 7g
Carbohydrates: 16g
Protein: 10g

Chicken Wing Drumettes

Prep Time: 10 minutes/ Cook Time 47 minutes/ Serves: 4

Ingredients:

- 1 tablespoon fresh chives, chopped
- 2 tablespoons unsalted roasted peanuts, chopped
- 1 garlic clove, chopped
- 3/8 teaspoon crushed red pepper
- 1 tablespoon roasted sesame oil
- 1 tablespoon lower-sodium soy sauce
- 2 tablespoons unsalted chicken stock
- 3 tablespoons honey
- 1/4 cup of rice vinegar
- Cooking spray as needed
- 10 large chicken drumettes

Directions:

1. Spread the chicken in the two Air Fryer Baskets in an even layer and spray cooking spray on top.
2. Return the Air Fryer Baskets to the Air Fryer.
3. Select the Air Fryer mode for Zone 1 with 390 degrees F temperature and 47 minutes cooking time.
4. Press the MATCH COOK button to copy the settings for Zone 2.
5. Initiate cooking by pressing the START/PAUSE BUTTON.
6. Flip the chicken drumettes once cooked halfway through, then resume cooking.
7. During this time, mix soy sauce, honey, stock, vinegar, garlic, and crushed red pepper in a suitable saucepan and place it over medium-high heat to cook on a simmer.
8. Cook this sauce for 6 minutes with occasional stirring, then pours it into a medium-sized bowl.
9. Add Air fried drumettes and toss well to coat with the honey sauce.

10. Garnish with chives and peanuts.
11. Serve warm and fresh.

Nutrition Contents:

Calories: 248
Fat: 15g
Carbohydrates: 15g
Protein: 24g

Feisty Bang Chicken

Prep Time: 10 minutes/ Cook Time 20 minutes/ Serves: 4

Ingredients:

- 2 green onions, chopped
- 1 and 1/2 cups panko bread crumbs
- 1 pound boneless chicken breast, diced
- 1/3 cup flour
- 2 tablespoons Sriracha sauce
- 1/2 cup sweet chili sauce
- 1 cup mayonnaise

Directions:

1. Mix mayonnaise with Sriracha and sweet chili sauce in a large bowl.
2. Keep 3/4 cup of the mixture aside.
3. Add flour, chicken, breadcrumbs, and remaining mayo mixture to a resealable plastic bag.
4. Zip the bag and shake well to coat.
5. Divide the chicken in the two Air fryer baskets in a single layer.
6. Return the Air Fryer Baskets to the Air Fryer.
7. Select the Air Fryer mode for Zone 1 with 390 degrees F temperature and 20 minutes cooking time.
8. Press the MATCH COOK button to copy the settings for Zone 2.
9. Initiate cooking by pressing the START/PAUSE BUTTON.
10. Flip the chicken once cooked halfway through.
11. Top the chicken with reserved mayo sauce.
12. Garnish with green onions and serve warm.

Nutrition Contents:

Calories: 400
Fat: 16g
Carbohydrates: 4g
Protein: 48g

Bacon-Wrapped Chicken Thighs

Prep Time: 10 minutes/ Cook Time 28 minutes/ Serves: 4

Ingredients:

- 2 teaspoons garlic, minced
- 1 and 1/2 pounds boneless skinless chicken thighs
- 1/3 pound thick cut-bacon
- 1 pinch black pepper, ground
- 1/8 teaspoon coarse salt
- 1/4 teaspoon dried basil
- 1/4 teaspoon dried thyme
- 1/2 garlic clove, minced
- 1/2 stick butter, soft

Directions:

1. Mix garlic softened butter with thyme, salt, basil, and black pepper in a bowl.
2. Add butter mixture on a piece of wax paper and roll it up tightly to make a butter log.
3. Place the log in the refrigerator for 2 hours.
4. Spray one bacon strip on a piece of wax paper.
5. Place each chicken thigh on top of one bacon strip and rub it with garlic.
6. Make a slit in the chicken thigh and add a tsp of butter to the chicken.
7. Wrap the bacon around the chicken thigh.
8. Repeat those same steps with all the chicken thighs.
9. Place the bacon-wrapped chicken thighs in the two Air Fryer Baskets.
10. Return the Air Fryer Baskets to the Air Fryer.
11. Select the Air Fryer mode for Zone 1 with 390 degrees F temperature and 28 minutes cooking time.
12. Press the MATCH COOK button to copy the settings for Zone 2.
13. Initiate cooking by pressing the START/PAUSE BUTTON.

14. Flip the chicken once cooked halfway through, and resume cooking.
15. Serve warm.

Nutrition Contents:

Calories: 457
Fat: 20g
Carbohydrates: 20g
Protein: 32g

Chapter 5: Vegan And Vegetable Recipes

Awesome Beets

Prep Time: 10 minutes/ Cook Time 10 minutes/ Serves: 6

Ingredients:

- 8 whole beets
- 2 tablespoon balsamic vinegar
- 2 tablespoon olive oil
- Salt and pepper to taste
- 4 springs rosemary

Directions:

1. Wash your beets and peel them
2. Cut beets into cubes
3. Take a bowl and mix in rosemary, pepper, salt, vinegar
4. Cover beets with the prepared sauce
5. Coat the beets with olive oil
6. Heat up the temperature of Zone 1 to 400 degrees F, set timer to 10 minutes
7. Select MATCH COOK to copy settings from Zone 1 to Zone 2
8. Transfer to Air Fryer cooking baskets and cook for 10 minutes
9. Serve with your cheese sauce, and enjoy!

Nutrition Contents:

Calories: 149
Fat: 1g
Carbohydrates: 5g
Protein: 30g

Hearty Fried Tomatoes

Prep Time: 10 minutes/ Cook Time 10 minutes/ Serves: 4

Ingredients:

- 4 green tomato
- 1/2 tablespoon Creole seasoning
- Salt and pepper to taste
- 1/2 cup almond flour
- 1 cup buttermilk
- Bread crumbs as needed

Directions:

1. Add flour to your plate and take another plate and add buttermilk
2. Cut tomatoes and season with salt and pepper
3. Make a mix of creole seasoning and crumbs
4. Take tomato slice and cover with flour, place in buttermilk and then into crumbs
5. Repeat with all tomatoes
6. Set the temperature of Zone 1 to 400 degrees F, and timer to 5 minutes
7. Select MATCH COOK and
8. Cook the tomato slices for 5 minutes
9. Serve with basil and enjoy!

Nutrition Contents:

Calories: 166
Fat: 12g
Carbohydrates: 11g
Protein: 3g

Tempeh Cheddar Mushrooms

Prep Time: 10 minutes/ Cook Time 8-10 minutes/ Serves: 4

Ingredients:

- 14 mushroom caps
- 1 tablespoon parsley, chopped
- 1 tablespoon olive oil
- 1/4 cup cheddar, grated
- 4 slices tempeh, chopped
- Salt and pepper to taste
- 1 garlic clove, minced

Directions:

1. Preheat on Air Fry function to 390 F.
2. In a bowl, add olive oil, tempeh, cheddar cheese, parsley, salt, pepper, and garlic.
3. Mix well with a spoon. Fill the mushroom caps with the tempeh mixture.
4. Set the temperature of Zone 1 to 390 degrees F, set the timer to 8 minutes
5. Select MATCH COOK to copy information of Zone 1 to Zone 2
6. Place the stuffed mushrooms in the baskets and fit in the baking tray; cook for 8 minutes.
7. Once golden and crispy, plate them and serve with a green salad.

Nutritional Contents:

Calories: 405
Fat: 11g
Carbohydrates: 57g
Protein: 23g

Mozzarella Eggplant Patties

Prep Time: 10 minutes/ Cook Time 5-10 minutes/ Serves: 4

Ingredients:

- 1 pickle, sliced
- 1/2 tablespoon tomato sauce
- 1 lettuce leaf
- 1 red onion, cut into rings
- 1 mozzarella slice, chopped
- 1 eggplant, sliced
- 1 hamburger bun

Directions:

1. Set the temperature of Zone 1 to 330 degrees F, set the timer to 6 minutes
2. Select MATCH COOK to copy information of Zone 1 to Zone 2
3. Place the eggplant slices in a greased baking tray and cook for 6 minutes.
4. Take out the tray, top the eggplant with mozzarella cheese and cook for 30 more seconds—spread tomato sauce on one half of the bun.
5. Place the lettuce leaf on top of the sauce. Place the cheesy eggplant on top of the lettuce.
6. Top with onion rings and pickles and then with the other bun half to serve.

Nutritional Contents:

Calories: 562
Fat: 25g
Carbohydrates: 41g
Protein: 48g

Breadcrumb Mushrooms

Prep Time: 10 minutes/ Cook Time 25 minutes/ Serves: 4

Ingredients:

- 16 small button mushrooms, stemmed and gills removed
- 1 garlic clove; crushed
- 1-1/2 spelt bread slices
- 1 tbsp. flat-leaf parsley, finely chopped
- 1-1/2 tbsp. olive oil
- Salt and ground black pepper; as your liking

Directions:

1. In a food processor, add the bread slices and pulse until fine crumbs form. Transfer the crumbs into a bowl. Add the garlic, parsley, salt, and black pepper and stir to combine.
2. Stir in the olive oil.
3. Set temperature of Zone 1 to 390 degrees F, set the timer to 10 minutes
4. Select MATCH COOK to copy Zone 1 information to Zone 2
5. Stuff each mushroom cap with the breadcrumbs mixture.
6. Arrange mushroom caps into the prepared air fryer baskets. Air fry for about 9 to 10 minutes.
7. Remove from the air fryer and transfer the mushrooms onto a serving platter.
8. Set aside to cool slightly. Serve warm.

Nutrition Contents:

Calories: 361
Fat: 2g
Carbohydrates: 75g
Protein: 10g

Extreme Hasselback Potatoes

Prep Time: 10 minutes/ Cook Time 25 minutes/ Serves: 4

Ingredients:

- 1 tablespoon fresh parsley, chopped
- Salt and pepper to taste
- 1/2 teaspoon ground paprika
- 3 garlic cloves, crushed
- 1 tablespoon olive oil
- 3 tablespoon butter, melted
- 4 medium Yukon Gold potatoes

Directions:

1. Slice each potato from the top to make 1/4-inch slices without cutting its 1/2-inch bottom, keeping the potato's bottom intact.
2. Mix butter with olive oil, garlic, and paprika in a small bowl.
3. Brush the garlic mixture on top of each potato and add the mixture into the slits.
4. Season them with salt and black pepper.
5. Place 2 seasoned potatoes in each of the Air Fryer Baskets
6. Return the Air Fryer Baskets to the Air Fryer.
7. Select the Air Fryer mode for Zone 1 with 375 degrees F temperature and 25 minutes cooking time.
8. Press the MATCH COOK button to copy the settings for Zone 2.
9. Initiate cooking by pressing the START/PAUSE BUTTON.
10. Brushing the potatoes again with butter mixture after 15 minutes, then resume cooking.
11. Garnish with parsley.
12. Serve warm.

Nutritional Contents:

Calories: 362
Fat: 10g
Carbohydrates: 48g
Protein: 5g

Awesome Zucchini Fritters

Prep Time: 10 minutes/ Cook Time 17 minutes/ Serves: 4

Ingredients:

- Yogurt tahini sauce for serving
- Salt and pepper to taste
- 2 teaspoons olive oil
- 2 garlic, minced
- 2 tablespoons chickpea flour
- 1 medium potato, cooked
- 1 cup corn kernel
- 2 medium zucchinis, grated

Directions:

1. Mix grated zucchini with a pinch of salt in a colander and leave them for 15 minutes.
2. Squeeze out their excess water.
3. Mash the cooked potato in a large-sized bowl with a fork.
4. Add zucchini, corn, garlic, chickpea flour, salt, and black pepper to the bowl.
5. Mix these fritters' ingredients together and make 2 tbsp. -sized balls out of this mixture and flatten them lightly.
6. Divide the fritters in the two Air Fryer baskets in a single layer and spray them with cooking.
7. Return the Air Fryer Baskets to the Air Fryer.
8. Select the Air Fryer mode for Zone 1 with 390 degrees F temperature and 17 minutes cooking time.
9. Press the MATCH COOK button to copy the settings for Zone 2.
10. Initiate cooking by pressing the START/PAUSE BUTTON.
11. Flip the fritters once cooked halfway through, then resume cooking.
12. Serve.

Nutritional Contents:

Calories: 340
Fat: 14g
Carbohydrates: 33g
Protein: 20g

Lovely Air Fried Okra

Prep Time: 10 minutes/ Cook Time 13 minutes/ Serves: 4

Ingredients:

- 1/8 teaspoon ground black pepper
- 1/4 teaspoon salt
- 1 teaspoon olive oil
- 1/2 pound okra pods sliced

Directions:

1. Preheat your Air Fryer Machine to 350 F.
2. Toss okra with olive oil, salt, and black pepper in a bowl.
3. Spread the okra in a single layer in the two Air Fryer Baskets.
4. Return the Air Fryer Baskets to the Air Fryer.
5. Select the Air Fryer mode for Zone 1 with 375 degrees F temperature and 13 minutes cooking time.
6. Press the MATCH COOK button to copy the settings for Zone 2.
7. Initiate cooking by pressing the START/PAUSE BUTTON.
8. Toss the okra once cooked halfway through, and resume cooking.
9. Serve warm.

Nutritional Contents:

Calories: 188
Fat: 1g
Carbohydrates: 15g
Protein: 6g

Creative Gingered Carrots

Prep Time: 10 minutes/ Cook Time 25 minutes/ Serves: 4

Ingredients:

- 1/2 teaspoon sesame seeds, garnish
- 1/2 tablespoons scallions, chopped
- 1/2 teaspoon garlic, minced
- 1/2 tablespoon soy sauce
- 1/2 tablespoon ginger, minced
- 1 tablespoon sesame oil
- 1 pound cup carrots, cut into chunks

Directions:

1. Toss all the ginger carrots ingredients, except the sesame seeds and scallions, in a suitable bowl.
2. Divide the carrots in the two Air Fryer Baskets in a single layer.
3. Return the Air Fryer Baskets to the Air Fryer.
4. Select the Air Fryer mode for Zone 1 with 390 degrees F temperature and 25 minutes cooking time.
5. Press the MATCH COOK button to copy the settings for Zone 2.
6. Initiate cooking by pressing the START/PAUSE BUTTON.
7. Toss the carrots once cooked halfway through.
8. Garnish with sesame seeds and scallions.
9. Serve warm.

Nutritional Contents:

Calories: 327
Fat: 31g
Carbohydrates: 49g
Protein: 13g

Tender Air Fried Tofu

Prep Time: 10 minutes/ Cook Time 14 minutes/ Serves: 4

Ingredients:

- 2/3 cup lime juice
- 6 tablespoons sesame oil, toasted
- 2 (14 ounces) pack extra-firm, water-packed tofu, drained
- 2/3 cup coconut aminos

Directions:

1. Pat dry the tofu bars and slice into half-inch cubes.
2. Toss all the remaining ingredients in a small bowl.
3. Marinate for 4 hours in the refrigerator. Drain off the excess water.
4. Divide the tofu cubes in the two Air Fryer baskets.
5. Return the Air Fryer Baskets to the Air Fryer.
6. Select the Air Fryer mode for Zone 1 with 400 degrees F temperature and 14 minutes cooking time.
7. Press the MATCH COOK button to copy the settings for Zone 2.
8. Initiate cooking by pressing the START/PAUSE BUTTON.
9. Toss the tofu once cooked halfway through, then resume cooking.
10. Serve warm.

Nutritional Contents:

Calories: 295
Fat: 3g
Carbohydrates: 10g
Protein: 1g

Chapter 6: Stew Recipes

Awesome Sea Bass Stew

Prep Time: 10 minutes/ Cook Time 20 minutes/ Serves: 4

Ingredients:

- 10 ounces white rice
- 4 ounces peas
- 2 red bell pepper, chopped
- 28 ounces white wine
- 6 ounces of water
- 3 pounds sea bass fillets, skinless, boneless, and cubed
- 8 shrimp
- Salt and black pepper to taste
- 2 tablespoon olive oil

Directions:

1. In your air fryer's pan, mix all ingredients and toss.
2. Set the temperature of Zone 1 to 400 degrees F, set the timer to 20 minutes, and set the mode to Air Fryer
3. MATCH COOK to copy information of Zone 1 to Zone 2
4. Place the pans in your air fryer baskets and cook at 400 degrees F for 20 minutes, stirring halfway.
5. Divide into bowls, serve, and enjoy.

Nutritional Contents:

Calories: 280
Fat: 12g
Carbohydrates: 16g
Protein: 11g

Hearty Orange Stew

Prep Time: 10 minutes/ Cook Time 20 minutes/ Serves: 4

Ingredients:

- 4 oranges, peeled and cut into segments
- 2-1/4 cups white sugar
- 2 cups orange juice

Directions:

1. In a pan that fits your air fryer, mix the oranges with the sugar and orange juice; toss.
2. Set Zone 1 temperature to 320 degrees F. set the timer to 20 minutes
3. Select MATCH COOK to copy information of Zone 1 to Zone 2
4. Place the pan in the fryer and cook at 320 degrees F for 20 minutes.
5. Divide the orange stew into cups, refrigerate, and serve cold.

Nutritional Contents:

Calories: 171
Fat: 1g
Carbohydrates: 8g
Protein: 2g

Chinese Pork Bites

Prep Time: 10 minutes/ Cook Time 12 minutes/ Serves: 4

Ingredients:

- 2 eggs
- 2 pounds pork stew meat, cubed
- 1 cup cornstarch
- 1 teaspoon sesame oil
- Salt and black pepper to taste
- 1/4 teaspoon Chinese five-spice
- 3 tablespoons olive oil

Directions:

1. In a bowl, add the Chinese spice, salt, pepper, and cornstarch; mix well.
2. In another bowl, mix the eggs and sesame oil; whisk.
3. Dredge the pork cubes in the cornstarch mix, then dip them in the egg mix.
4. Set the temperature of Zone 1 to 360 degrees F and set the timer to 12 minutes
5. Select MATCH COOK to copy information of Zone 1 to Zone 2
6. Transfer the prepared pork meat between the cooking baskets and let them cook
7. Divide into bowls and, if desired, serve with a side salad
8. Enjoy!

Nutritional Contents:

Calories: 270
Fat: 8g
Carbohydrates: 16g
Protein: 5g

Autumn Stew

Prep Time: 10 minutes/ Cook Time: 10-14 minutes/ Serves: 6

Ingredients:

- 6 tablespoon avocado oil
- 2 white onion, chopped
- 12 white mushrooms, quartered
- 1 tablespoon oregano
- 6 cups Sebi friendly vegetable stock
- Pinch of salt
- 4 zucchinis, chopped
- 2 tablespoon spelt flour

Directions:

1. Set the temperature of Zone 1 to 300 degrees F and set the timer to 10 minutes
2. Select MATCH COOK to copy Zone 1 information to Zone 2
3. Add oil to your cooking basket
4. Add onion, zucchini, mushrooms, oregano and cook for 3 minutes
5. Add spelt flour and stir well until thick
6. Add stock, salt divide the mixture between the baskets
7. Cook for 10 minutes more
8. Once done, serve and enjoy

Nutritional Contents:

Calories: 117
Fat: 6g
Carbohydrates: 17g
Protein: 3g

Creative Paprika Pork

Prep Time: 10 minutes/ Cook Time 25 minutes/ Serves: 4

Ingredients:

- 2-pound pork stew meat, cubed
- 8 teaspoons sweet paprika
- Pinch of salt and pepper
- 2 cup coconut cream
- 2 tablespoon butter, melted
- 2 tablespoon parsley, chopped

Directions:

1. Take a pan and place it over medium heat, add a bit of oil and brown pork for 5 minutes
2. Add remaining ingredients to the pan and toss well
3. Set your Air Fryer Zone 1 to 390 degrees F, set the timer to 20 minutes
4. MATCH COOK to copy information of Zone 1 to Zone 2
5. Divide the mix between the cooking pans
6. Cook for 20 minutes
7. Divide and enjoy!

Nutritional Contents:

Calories: 273
Fat: 12g
Carbohydrates: 6g
Protein: 20g

Feisty Indian Pork Curry

Prep Time: 10 minutes/ Cook Time 30 minutes/ Serves: 5

Ingredients:

- 2-pound pork stew meat, cubed
- 4 ounces coconut cream
- 6 tablespoons pure cream
- 6 tablespoons curry powder
- 4 tablespoons olive oil
- 2 yellow onion, chopped
- 2 tablespoon cilantro, chopped
- Salt and black pepper to taste

Directions:

1. In a bowl, mix the pork with the curry powder, salt, and pepper.
2. Heat up a pan that fits your air fryer with the oil over medium-high heat; add the pork, toss, and brown for 3 minutes.
3. Add the coconut cream, pure cream, and onions; toss.
4. MATCH COOK to copy information of Zone 1 to Zone 2
5. Transfer pan to the Air Fryer cooking baskets, divide them equally
6. Add the cilantro and toss.
7. Divide everything into bowls and serve.

Nutritional Contents:

Calories: 271
Fat: 8g
Carbohydrates: 18g
Protein: 18g

Cauliflower And Pork Total Stew

Prep Time: 10 minutes/ Cook Time 22 minutes/ Serves: 4

Ingredients:

- 2-pound pork stew meat, cubed
- 2 cauliflower head, florets separated
- 4 tablespoons olive oil
- 2 teaspoon soy sauce
- 2 teaspoon sugar
- 1/2 cup balsamic vinegar
- 2 garlic clove, minced

Directions:

1. Place all the ingredients in a pan that fits your air fryer and mix well.
2. Set the temperature of Air Fryer Zone 1 to 390 degrees F, set the timer to 22 minutes
3. Select MATCH COOK to copy information of Zone 1 to Zone 2
4. Transfer the mix to the cooking baskets and let them cook
5. Divide into bowls, serve, and enjoy.

Nutritional Contents:

Calories: 270
Fat: 10g
Carbohydrates: 23g
Protein: 20g

Awesome Rosemary Stew

Prep Time: 10 minutes/ Cook Time 15 minutes/ Serves: 4

Ingredients:

- 2 pounds beef roast
- 1 tablespoon olive oil
- 1 medium onion
- 1 teaspoon salt
- 2 teaspoons rosemary and thyme

Directions:

1. Place beef roast in Air Fryer cooking basket, rub it well with olive oil, rosemary, thyme, and onion
2. Set your temperature to 390 degrees F of Zone 1 with the timer set to 15 minutes
3. Select MATCH cook to copy Zone 1 information to Zone 2
4. Transfer the meat to Air Fryer cooking baskets
5. Let them cook until the timer runs out
6. Serve and enjoy!

Nutritional Contents:

Calories: 290
Fat: 14g
Carbohydrates: 8g
Protein: 32g

Beef And Plums Exotica

Prep Time: 10 minutes/ Cook Time 40 minutes/ Serves: 4

Ingredients:

- 1-1/2 pounds beef stew meat, cubed
- 3 tablespoons honey
- 2 tablespoons olive oil
- 9 ounces plums, pitted and halved
- 8 ounces beef stock
- 2 yellow onions, chopped
- 2 garlic cloves, minced
- Salt and black pepper to tastes
- 1 teaspoon turmeric powder
- 1 teaspoon ginger powder
- 1 teaspoon cinnamon powder

Directions:

1. In a pan that fits your air fryer, heats up the oil over medium heat.
2. Add the beef, stir, and brown for 2 minutes.
3. Add the honey, onions, garlic, salt, pepper, turmeric, ginger, and cinnamon; toss, and cook for 2-3 minutes more.
4. Add the plums and the stock; toss again.
5. Set Zone 1 temperature to 380 degrees F, set timer to 30 minutes
6. Transfer the pans to the Air Fryer baskets and let them cook until the timer runs out
7. Divide everything into bowls and serve.

Nutritional Contents:

Calories: 271
Fat: 11g
Carbohydrates: 20g
Protein: 20g

Perfect Rosemary Beef Stew

Prep Time: 10 minutes/ Cook Time 15 minutes/ Serves: 4

Ingredients:

- 4 pounds beef roast
- 2 tablespoon olive oil
- 2 medium onion
- 2 teaspoon salt
- 4 teaspoons rosemary and thyme

Directions:

1. Place beef roast in Air Fryer cooking basket, rub it well with olive oil, rosemary, thyme, and onion
2. Set temperature of Zone 1 to 390 degrees F and set timer to 15 minutes, set it to ROAST mode
3. Select MATCH COOK to copy information of Zone 1 to Zone 2
4. Transfer to your Air Fryer baskets
5. Let them cook and let the timer run out
6. Serve and enjoy!

Nutritional Contents:

Calories: 290
Fat: 14g
Carbohydrates: 8g
Protein: 32g

Chapter 7: Eggs And Beans Recipes

Meaty Zucchini Omelet

Prep Time: 10 minutes/ Cook Time 10 minutes/ Serves: 4

Ingredients:

- 8 whole eggs
- 1/2 cup milk
- Salt and pepper to taste
- 1 cup cooked chicken, chopped
- 1 cup cheddar cheese, shredded
- 1/2 cup fresh chives, chopped
- 3/4 cup zucchini, chopped

Directions:

1. In a bowl, add the eggs, milk, salt, and black pepper and beat well. Add the remaining ingredients and stir to combine.
2. Place the mixture into a greased baking pan.
3. Set Zone 1 temperature to 315 degrees F and set the timer to 35 minutes; select AIR FRY mode
4. MATCH COOK to copy information of Zone 1 to Zone 2
5. When the unit beeps to show that it is preheated, open the lid. Transfer the baking pan between the baskets
6. Let them cook until the timer runs out
7. Cut into equal-sized wedges and serve hot.

Nutritional Contents:

Calories: 207
Fat: 13g
Carbohydrates: 2g
Protein: 10g

Bread Omelet Cup

Prep Time: 10 minutes/ Cook Time 10 minutes/ Serves: 8

Ingredients:

- 8 crusty rolls (3-by-4-inch)
- 10 eggs
- Pinch salt
- 1 teaspoon thyme, dried
- 4 tablespoons heavy cream
- 6 strips precooked bacon, chopped
- 8 Gouda or Swiss cheese mini wedges, thin slices

Directions:

1. Set your temperature to Zone 1 to 330 degrees F, set cooking mode to BAKE, and timer to 12 minutes
2. Select MATCH COOK to copy information of Zone 1 to Zone 2
3. Cut the tops off the rolls and remove the inside with your fingers.
4. Make a shell with about 1/2-inch of bread remaining.
5. Line the rolls with a slice of cheese and gently pressing down so the cheese conforms to the inside of the roll.
6. Take a medium-sized bowl and beat the eggs with the heavy cream until combined.
7. Stir in the bacon, thyme, salt, and pepper.
8. Fill the egg mixture into the rolls over the cheese.
9. Transfer them to the baking baskets
10. Bake for 8 to 12 minutes or until the eggs are puffed and golden brown.
11. Enjoy!

Nutritional Contents:

Calories: 499
Fat: 24g
Carbohydrates: 46g
Protein: 26g

Veggie Baked Eggs

Prep Time: 10 minutes/ Cook Time 10 minutes/ Serves: 4

Ingredients:

- 1/4 teaspoon dried oregano
- 1/2 teaspoon dried basil
- 1/4 teaspoon onion powder
- 1/4 teaspoon garlic powder
- 2 tablespoons salted butter
- 2 large eggs
- 1/2 medium green bell pepper, seeded and diced
- 1 medium Roma tomatoes, diced
- 1 small zucchini, sliced, quartered
- 1 cup fresh spinach, chopped

Directions:

1. Grease two: 4-inch ramekins with 1 tbsp. Butter each.
2. Take a large bowl, toss zucchini, bell pepper, spinach, and tomatoes. Divide the mixture into two and place half in each ramekin.
3. Crack an egg on top of each ramekin and sprinkle with onion powder, garlic powder, basil, and oregano.
4. Set the temperature of Zone 1 to 330 degrees F, set AIR FRY mode, and set the timer to 10 minutes
5. Transfer them to your Air Fryer cooking baskets
6. Serve and enjoy once done!

Nutrition Contents:

Calories: 96
Fat: 7g
Carbohydrates: 10g
Protein: 4g

The Best Left-Over Mac

Prep Time: 10 minutes/ Cook Time 20 minutes/ Serves: 4

Ingredients:

- 8 tablespoons leftover macaroni with cheese
- Extra cheese for serving
- Pastry
- Salt and pepper to taste
- 1 teaspoon garlic puree
- 2 tablespoon Greek yogurt
- 2 whole eggs
- 11 and 3/4 ounces of milk

Directions:

1. Set the temperature of Zone 1 to 360 degrees F, set the timer to 20 minutes, and set it to AIR FRY mode
2. Select MATCH COOK to copy Zone 1 information to Zone 2
3. Mix mac with cheese and flour.
4. Form shells using the pastry.
5. Take a bowl and mix in yogurt, garlic, and cheese.
6. Add egg with milk the cheese mixture.
7. Add macaroni, milk mix to your prepared shell and close it gently.
8. Divide the mix between Air Fryer baskets
9. Cook for 20 minutes.
10. Serve and enjoy!

Nutritional Contents:

Calories: 279
Fat: 2g
Carbohydrates: 21g
Protein: 47g

Lovely Tomato Frittata

Prep Time: 10 minutes/ Cook Time 10 minutes/ Serves: 8

Ingredients:

- Salt as needed
- 2 cup Gouda cheese, shredded
- 1 cup milk
- 1 cup tomatoes, chopped
- 8 whole eggs

Directions:

1. In a small baking pan, add all the ingredients and mix well.
2. The select temperature of Zone 1 to 340 degrees F and Set timer to 30 minutes
3. MATCH COOK to copy information of Zone 1 to Zone 2
4. Select AIR FRY Mode and transfer the mixture between the cooking baskets (greased)
5. Let them cook well
6. Cut into 2 wedges and serve.

Nutritional Contents:

Calories: 247
Fat: 16g
Carbohydrates: 8g
Protein: 18g

Avocado Egg Cups

Prep Time: 10 minutes/ Cook Time 10 minutes/ Serves: 4

Ingredients:

- 4 cooked bacon slices, crumbled
- Salt and pepper to taste
- 4 large whole eggs
- 2 avocados, halved and pitted

Directions:

1. Carefully scoop out about 2 teaspoons of flesh from each avocado half.
2. Crack 1 egg in each avocado half and sprinkle with salt and black pepper.
3. Set Zone 1 temperature to 375 degrees F, set timer to 10 minutes
4. Select Roast mode, select MATCH COOK to copy Zone 1 information to Zone 2
5. Grease the Air Fryer baskets
6. Transfer Avocado Halves to the baskets and let them cook
7. Top each avocado half with bacon pieces and serve.

Nutritional Contents:

Calories: 300
Fat: 26g
Carbohydrates: 9g
Protein: 10g

Baked Green Beans

Prep Time: 10 minutes/ Cook Time 15-20 minutes/ Serves: 6

Ingredients:

- 2 cup panko
- 4 whole eggs
- 1 cup parmesan
- 1 cup flour
- Cayenne pepper
- 3 pounds green beans
- Salt to taste

Directions:

1. Set your temperature of Zone 1 to 400 degrees F, set the timer to 15 minutes
2. Select MATCH COOK to copy Zone 1 settings to Zone 2, select AIR FRY mode
3. Take a bowl and mix in panko, parmesan cheese, cayenne pepper
4. Season with salt, pepper to the cheese mix
5. Cover beans with flour, then dredge the beans into the egg mix.
6. Finally, dredge the beans into the parmesan-panko mix
7. Transfer beans to Air Fryer cooking baskets and cook for 15 minutes
8. Serve and enjoy with any remaining sauce!

Nutritional Contents:

Calories: 34
Fat: 2g
Carbohydrates: 8g
Protein: 22g

Cups -O Ham Quiche

Ingredients:

- 5 whole eggs
- 2 and 1/4 ounces ham
- 1 cup milk
- 1/8 teaspoon pepper
- 1 and 1/2 cup Swiss cheese
- 1/4 teaspoon salt
- 1/4 cup Green onion
- 1/2 teaspoon thyme

Directions:

1. Set the Zone 1 temperature to 350 degrees F, Set a timer to 15 minutes, and select BAKE mode
2. Choose MATCH COOK to copy Zone 1 information to Zone 2
3. Crack your eggs in a bowl and beat it well.
4. Add thyme onion, salt, Swiss cheese pepper, milk to the beaten eggs.
5. Prepare your baking forms for muffins and place ham slices in each baking form.
6. Cover the ham with egg mixture.
7. Transfer to Air Fryer and bake for 15 minutes.
8. Serve and enjoy!

Nutritional Contents:

Calories: 80
Fat: 5g
Carbohydrates: 0g
Protein: 7g

Cool Feta Quiche

Prep Time: 10 minutes/ Cook Time 40 minutes/ Serves: 6

Ingredients:

- 12 ounces thawed puff pastry
- 4 large eggs
- 1/4 cup milk
- 1 medium zucchini, sliced
- 4 ounces feta, drained and crumbled
- 2 tablespoons fresh dill, chopped
- Olive oil spray as needed
- Salt and pepper as needed

Directions:

1. Preheat your Air Fryer to a temperature of 360-degree Fahrenheit
2. Set Zone 1 temperature to 360 degrees F and time to 20 minutes
3. Select MATCH COOK to copy Zone 1 information to Zone 2
4. Take a bowl and beat in eggs
5. Season the egg with salt and pepper
6. Add zucchini, feta cheese, and dill
7. Give it a stir
8. Take 8 muffin tins and grease them well
9. Roll out your pastry and cover the bottom and sides of your muffin tin with the pastry
10. Pour the egg mix amongst the muffins and cook them by dividing between the baskets
11. Cook until you have a golden crust
12. Transfer them to your serving plate and enjoy!

Nutritional Contents:

Calories: 140
Fat: 8g
Carbohydrates: 11g
Protein: 4g

Sausage And Cheese Chard Quiche

Prep Time: 10 minutes/ Cook Time 20 minutes/ Serves: 4

Ingredients:

- Swiss chard; chopped -8 cups
- Onion; chopped -1/2 cup
- Parmesan; grated-1/4 cup
- Eggs-3
- Ricotta cheese-2 cups
- Mozzarella; shredded-1 cup
- Sausage; chopped -1-pound
- Olive oil -1 tbsps
- Garlic clove; minced -1
- Salt and black pepper -to the taste
- Nutmeg- A pinch

Directions:

1. Take a baking dish suitable to fit in your air fryer cooking baskets
2. Add oil to this pan and place it over medium heat.
3. Toss in garlic, onions, chard, salt, nutmeg, pepper, and saute for 2 minutes.
4. Whisk eggs with ricotta, mozzarella, and parmesan in a separate bowl.
5. Pour this mixture over the chard mixture.
6. Toss well, then place the dish in the air fryer basket and seal it.
7. Set the Zone 1 temperature to 320 degrees F, set timer to 17 minutes
8. Cook them for 17 minutes at 320 F on Air fryer mode.
9. Enjoy warm.

Nutritional Contents:

Calories: 280
Fat: 12g
Carbohydrates: 16g
Protein: 11

Chapter 8: Desserts And Snacks Recipes

Nutty Banana Muffin

Prep Time: 10 minutes/ Cook Time 20-25 minutes/ Serves: 4

Ingredients:

- 1 and 1/2 cups Teff Flour
- 1/2 teaspoon salt
- 3/4 cup date syrup
- 2 medium pureed burro bananas
- 1/4 cup Grapeseed oil
- 3/4 cup walnut milk
- 1 tablespoon key lime juice
- 1/2 cup chopped walnuts
- 1 burro banana, chopped

Directions:

1. Preheat your Air Fryer 385 degrees F
2. Set your Zone 1 temperature to 385 degrees F, Select timer to 20-25 minutes, and select BAKE mode
3. Select MATCH COOK and to copy Zone 1 information to Zone 2
4. Take a muffin tray and grease 12 cups with liners
5. Take a large bowl and add dry ingredients, mix well
6. Add wet ingredients to another bowl and mix well with pureed bananas
7. Take the two bowls and pour the mixture into one large bowl; mix well
8. Add chopped burro banana and walnuts

9. Pour batter into muffin tins
10. Transfer to Air Fryer cooking baskets, bake for 20-25 minutes until golden brown
11. Let them cool for 10 minutes
12. Serve and enjoy!

Nutritional Contents:

Calories: 217
Fat: 42g
Carbohydrates: 42g
Protein: 2g

Lovely Quinoa Bread

Prep Time: 10 minutes/ Cook Time 30-40 minutes/ Serves: 4

Ingredients:

- 2 and 1/2 cups uncooked quinoa, soaked and overnight, rinsed
- 1/2 cup sesame seeds
- 1 teaspoon baking soda
- 1/2 teaspoon salt
- 1/2 cup olive oil
- 1 cup of sparkling water
- 2 tablespoons fresh lemon juice

Directions:

1. Set Zone 1 temperature to 300 degrees F, set timer to 40 minutes, and set it to BAKE mode
2. Select MATCH COOK mode to copy Zone 1 information to Zone 2
3. Line loaf pan with parchment paper
4. Take a food processor and add all ingredients, pulse well
5. Transfer into two separate pans and divide them between the cooking baskets
6. Cook for 30-40 minutes until a toothpick comes clean
7. Remove pan from Fryer and keep in the cooling rack, let it cool
8. Serve and enjoy!

Nutritional Contents:

Calories: 137
Fat: 7g
Carbohydrates: 16g
Protein: 14g

Berry Zucchini Pudding

Prep Time: 10 minutes/ Cook Time: 20-25 minutes/ Serves: 4

Ingredients:

- 3 cups zucchini, chopped
- 2 apples, rinsed and juiced
- 1/3 cup chia seeds
- 1/2 cup blueberries, juiced
- 1 tablespoon agave
- 2 tablespoons sparkling water
- 1 tablespoon coconut flakes

Directions:

1. Preheat your Air Fryer to 350 degrees F
2. Set temperature to 350 degrees F of Zone 1 and set the timer to 25 minutes; choose BAKE mode
3. Select MATCH COOK to copy Zone 1 information to Zone 2
4. Take two casserole dishes small enough to fit inside the cooking basket
5. Add zucchini and apple juice to the dish
6. Bake for 20-25 minutes
7. Stir in blueberry juice, chia seeds, agave and stir
8. Let it sit for 10 minutes
9. Blend the mixture until smooth
10. Serve with garnish coconut flakes, serve and enjoy!

Nutritional Contents:

Calories: 102
Fat: 2g
Carbohydrates: 20g
Protein: 1.3g

Hot But Cool Banana Dessert

Prep Time: 10 minutes/ Cook Time 10 minutes/ Serves: 4

Ingredients:

- 1 tablespoon sugar
- 2 teaspoons baking powder
- 4 whole eggs, beaten
- 2 cups of water
- 6 tablespoons sesame seeds
- 2 teaspoons salt
- 10 bananas, sliced
- 3 cups flour

Directions:

1. Set the temperature of Zone 1 to 340 degrees F, Set a timer to 10 minutes, and mode to BAKE
2. In a bowl, mix salt, sesame seeds, flour, baking powder, eggs, sugar, and water.
3. Coat sliced bananas with the flour mixture. Place the prepared slices in the Air Fryer baskets and fit in the baking tray;
4. Cook for 8-10 minutes. Serve chilled.

Nutritional Contents:

Calories: 425
Fat: 20g
Carbohydrates: 59g
Protein: 9g

Blueberry Healthy Muffin

Prep Time: 10 minutes/ Cook Time 12-15 minutes/ Serves: 4

Ingredients:

- 1/2 sea salt
- 1/2 cup maple syrup
- 2 teaspoon baking powder
- 1 cup sea moss
- 1 and 1/2 cup spelt flour
- 1 and 1/2 cup Kamut flour
- 2 cup hemp milk
- 2 cup blueberries

Directions:

1. Set Zone 1 temperature to 380 degrees F, set timer to 20-25 minutes, and select BAKE mode
2. Choose MATCH COOK to copy settings of Zone 1 to Zone 2
3. Take your muffin tins and gently grease them
4. Take a bowl and add flour, syrup, salt, baking powder, seamless and mix well
5. Add milk and mix well
6. Fold in blueberries
7. Pour into muffin tins
8. Transfer to the cooking basket, bake for 20-25 minutes until nicely baked
9. Serve and enjoy!

Nutritional Contents:

Calories: 217
Fat: 10g
Carbohydrates: 32g
Protein: 4g

Hearty Miniature Apple Pies

Prep Time: 10 minutes/ Cook Time 25 minutes/ Serves: 6

Ingredients:

- 2 teaspoons milk
- 1/2 cup sugar, powdered
- 1 tablespoon grapeseed oil
- Cooking spray as needed
- 1 (14 ounces) package pastry, 9-inch crust pie
- 4 teaspoons cold water
- 2 teaspoons cornstarch
- 4 medium Granny Smith apples, diced
- 2 teaspoons cinnamon, ground
- 12 tablespoons brown sugar
- 8 tablespoons butter, softened

Directions:

1. Toss apples with brown sugar, butter, and cinnamon in a suitable skillet.
2. Place the skillet over medium heat and stir cook for 5 minutes.
3. Mix cornstarch with cold water in a small bowl.
4. Add cornstarch mixture into the apple and cook for 1 minute until it thickens.
5. Remove this filling from the heat and allow it to cool.
6. Unroll the pie crust and spray on a floured surface.
7. Cut the dough into 16 equal rectangles.
8. Wet the edges of the 8 rectangles with water and divide the apple filling at the center of these rectangles.
9. Place the other 8 rectangles on top and crimp the edges with a fork.
10. Place 4 small pies in each of the Air Fryer Baskets.
11. Return the Air Fryer Baskets to the Air Fryer.
12. Select the Air Fryer mode for Zone 1 with 390 degrees F temperature

and 17 minutes cooking time.

13. Press the MATCH COOK button to copy the settings for Zone 2.
14. Initiate cooking by pressing the START/PAUSE BUTTON.
15. Flip the pies once cooked halfway through, and resume cooking.
16. Meanwhile, mix sugar with milk.
17. Pour this mixture over the apple pies.
18. Serve fresh.

Nutrition Contents:

Calories: 271
Fat: 15g
Carbohydrates: 33g
Protein: 3g

Feisty Crispy Beignets

Prep Time: 10 minutes/ Cook Time 17 minutes/ Serves: 6

Ingredients:

- 2 tablespoons confectioner's sugar
- 1 pinch salt
- 1/2 teaspoon vanilla powder
- 1/2 teaspoon vanilla extract
- 1 and 1/2 teaspoon butter, melted
- 1 large egg, melted
- 1/2 cup all-purpose flour
- 1/8 cup water
- 1/4 cup white sugar
- Cooking spray as needed

Directions:

1. Beat flour with water, sugar, egg yolk, baking powder, butter, vanilla extract, and salt in a large bowl until lumps-free.
2. Beat egg whites in a separate bowl and beat using an electric hand mixer until it forms soft peaks.
3. Add the egg white to the flour batter and mix gently until fully incorporated.
4. Divide the dough into small beignets and place them in the air fryer baskets.
5. Return the Air Fryer Baskets to the Air Fryer.
6. Select the Air Fryer mode for Zone 1 with 390 degrees F temperature and 17 minutes cooking time.
7. Press the MATCH COOK button to copy the settings for Zone 2.
8. Initiate cooking by pressing the START/PAUSE BUTTON.
9. And cook for another 4 minutes—Dust the cooked beignets with sugar.
10. Serve.

Nutrition Contents:

Calories: 212
Fat: 8g
Carbohydrates: 51g
Protein: 3g

Awesome Oat Crisps

Prep Time: 10 minutes/ Cook Time 14 minutes/ Serves: 6

Ingredients:

- 1/2 teaspoon cinnamon
- 2 tablespoon light butter, mete
- 1/4 cup brown sugar
- 1/3 cup quick oats
- 3 tablespoons all-purpose flour, divided
- 2 teaspoons lemon juice
- 1 tablespoon pure maple syrup
- 3 cups apples, chopped

Directions:

1. Toss the chopped apples with 1 tbsp all-purpose flour, cinnamon, maple syrup, and lemon juice in a suitable bowl.
2. Divide the apples in the two air fryer baskets with their crisper plates.
3. Whisk oats, brown sugar, and remaining all-purpose flour in a small bowl.
4. Stir in melted butter, then divides this mixture over the apples.
5. Return the Air Fryer Baskets to the Air Fryer.
6. Select the Bake mode for Zone 1 with 375 degrees F temperature and 14 minutes cooking time.
7. Press the MATCH COOK button to copy the settings for Zone 2.
8. Initiate cooking by pressing the START/PAUSE BUTTON.
9. Enjoy fresh.

Nutrition Contents:

Calories: 264
Fat: 14g
Carbohydrates: 33g
Protein: 4g

Hearty Cinnamon Doughnuts

Prep Time: 10 minutes/ Cook Time 15 minutes/ Serves: 4

Ingredients:

- Melted butter to brush biscuits
- Coconut oil as needed
- 1/2 cup powdered sugar
- 1 teaspoon cinnamon
- 1/2 cup white sugar
- 1 can pre-made biscuit dough

Directions:

1. Place all the biscuits on a cutting board and cut holes in each biscuit center using a cookie cutter.
2. Grease the Air Fryer Baskets with coconut oil.
3. Place the biscuits in the two Air Fryers Baskets while keeping them 1 inch apart.
4. Return the Air Fryer Baskets to the Air Fryer.
5. Select the Air Fryer mode for Zone 1 with 375 degrees F temperature and 15 minutes cooking time.
6. Press the MATCH COOK button to copy the settings for Zone 2.
7. Initiate cooking by pressing the START/PAUSE BUTTON.
8. Brush all the donuts with melted butter and sprinkle cinnamon and sugar on top.
9. Air fry these donuts for one minute more.
10. Enjoy.

Nutrition Contents:

Calories: 282
Fat: 5g
Carbohydrates: 25g
Protein: 2g

Excellent Air Fried Bananas

Prep Time: 10 minutes/ Cook Time 13 minutes/ Serves: 6

Ingredients:

- 1 serving of avocado oil cooking spray
- 4 bananas, sliced into 1/8-inch-thick diagonals

Directions:

1. Spread the banana slices in the two air fryer baskets in a single layer.
2. Drizzle avocado oil over the banana slices.
3. Return the Air Fryer Baskets to the Air Fryer.
4. Select the Air Fryer mode for Zone 1 with 350 degrees F temperature and 13 minutes cooking time.
5. Press the MATCH COOK button to copy the settings for Zone 2.
6. Initiate cooking by pressing the START/PAUSE BUTTON.
7. Serve.

Nutrition Contents:

Calories: 171
Fat: 2g
Carbohydrates: 23g
Protein: 2g

Conclusion

I can't express how honored I am to think that you found my book interesting and informative enough to read it all through to the end.

Thank you again for purchasing this book, and I hope you had as much fun reading it as I had written it.

I bid you farewell and encourage you to move forward with your amazing Ninja Foodi 2 Basket Air Fryer!

Manufactured by Amazon.ca
Bolton, ON